Workshop on Speech and Language Processing Tools in Education

Held at the 24th International Conference on Computational Linguistics (COLING 2012)

Mumbai, India
15 December 2012

Editors:

Radhika Mamidi
Kishore Prahallad

ISBN: 978-1-62748-358-2

Printed from e-media with permission by:

Curran Associates, Inc.
57 Morehouse Lane
Red Hook, NY 12571

CURRAN ASSOCIATES INC. proceedings.com

Some format issues inherent in the e-media version may also appear in this print version.

Printed by Curran Associates, Inc. (2013)

Association for Computational Linguistics
209 N. Eighth Street
Stroudsburg, Pennsylvania 18360

Phone: 1-570-476-8006
Fax: 1-570-476-0860

acl@aclweb.org

Additional copies of this publication are available from:

Curran Associates, Inc.
57 Morehouse Lane
Red Hook, NY 12571 USA
Phone: 845-758-0400
Fax: 845-758-2634
Email: curran@proceedings.com
Web: www.proceedings.com

COLING 2012

24th International Conference on Computational Linguistics

Proceedings of the Workshop on Speech and Language Processing Tools in Education

Workshop chairs:
Radhika Mamidi and Kishore Prahallad

15 December 2012
Mumbai, India

Diamond sponsors

Tata Consultancy Services
Linguistic Data Consortium for Indian Languages (LDC-IL)

Gold Sponsors

Microsoft Research
Beijing Baidu Netcon Science Technology Co. Ltd.

Silver sponsors

IBM, India Private Limited
Crimson Interactive Pvt. Ltd.
Yahoo
Easy Transcription & Software Pvt. Ltd.

Proceedings of the Workshop on Speech and Language Processing Tools in Education
Radhika Mamidi and Kishore Prahallad (eds.)

Preface

Information and communication technology (ICT) along with conventional aids assumes a central role in today's classroom teaching. With the advent of Internet and WWW, accessing information and communication in the context of a learner-learner and a teacher-learner interaction has become more effective. The resources and tools on the WWW are considered to be one of the best available, specifically because of its 'anywhere, anytime' access. One of the most important domains in ICT is speech and language technologies. Tools and applications including text-to-speech, automatic speech recognition, spelling checkers, machine translation, and information retrieval/extraction systems have found their way into a common man's day-to-day life. However, there has been little progress in their use and application for educational purposes.

This workshop provided an opportunity for a discussion and exchange of ideas on multidisciplinary research in academia by bringing together technologies from different sub-areas of speech, language technologies, learning sciences and education.

We received a good response and based on referee reports, 12 papers were selected for presentations. There were equal number of papers from India and abroad covering a wide range of sub-areas.

We thank the members of Scientific Committee for their support and cooperation for the workshop. We also thank them for giving a thorough feedback to the authors. Finally, we thank the organizers of COLING 2012 for giving us the opportunity to conduct this workshop.

Radhika Mamidi
Kishore Prahallad

Workshop Committees

Scientific Committee

- Alan W Black, Carnegie Mellon University, USA
- Robert Elliott, University of Oregon, USA
- Maxine Eskenazi, Carnegie Mellon University, USA
- Shajith Ikbal, IBM Research, India
- Radhika Mamidi, IIIT Hyderabad, India
- Nobuaki Minematsu, The University of Tokyo, Japan
- Helen Ming, The Chinese University of Hong Kong, Hong Kong
- Kannan M Moudgalya, IIT Bombay, India
- Hema A Murthy, IIT Madras, India
- Kishore Prahallad, IIIT Hyderabad, India
- Martin Russell, University of Birmingham, UK
- Helmer Strik, Radboud University, Nijmegen, Netherlands
- Vasudeva Varma, IIIT Hyderabad, India
- Ashish Verma, IBM Research, India

Organizing Committee

- Radhika Mamidi (Chair), IIIT Hyderabad, India
- Kishore Prahallad (Co-Chair), IIIT Hyderabad, India

Table of Contents

Workshop on Speech and Language Processing Tools in Education

Program

Saturday, 15 December 2012

09:30–09:50	Introduction
09:50–11:30	**Presentations**
09:50–10:00	*Effective Mentor Suggestion System for Online Collaboration Platform* Advait Raut, Upasana Gaikwad, Ramakrishna Bairi and Ganesh Ramakrishnan
10:00–10:10	*Automatically Assessing Free Texts* Yllias Chali and Sadid A. Hasan
10:10–10:20	*Automatic pronunciation assessment for language learners with acoustic-phonetic features* Vaishali Patil and Preeti Rao
10:20–10:30	*An Issue-oriented Syllabus Retrieval System using Terminology-based Syllabus Structuring and Visualization* Hideki Mima
10:30–10:40	*Real-Time Tone Recognition in A Computer-Assisted Language Learning System for German Learners of Mandarin* Hussein Hussein, Hansjörg Mixdorff and Rüdiger Hoffmann
10:40–10:50	*Textbook Construction from Lecture Transcripts* Aliabbas Petiwala, Kannan Moudgalya and Pushpak Bhattacharya
10:50–11:00	*Enriching An Academic knowledge base using Linked Open Data* Chetana Gavankar, Ashish Kulkarni, Yuan-Fang Li and Ganesh Ramakrishnan
11:00–11:10	*Automatic Pronunciation Scoring And Mispronunciation Detection Using CMUSphinx* Ronanki Srikanth and James Salsman
11:10–11:20	*Content Bookmarking and Recommendation* Ananth Vyasarayamut, Satyabrata Behera and Ganesh Ramakrishnan
11:20–11:30	*A template matching approach for detecting pronunciation mismatch* Lavanya Prahallad, Radhika Mamidi and Kishore Prahallad
11:30–12:00	Tea break
12:00–13:30	**Poster Session/Demo**
13:30–14:30	Lunch

Effective Mentor Suggestion System for Collaborative Learning

Advait Raut[1] *Upasana G*[2] *Ramakrishna Bairi*[3] *Ganesh Ramakrishnan*[2]

(1) IBM, Bangalore, India, 560045

(2) IITB, Mumbai, India, 400076

(3) IITB-Monash Research Academy, Mumbai, India, 400076

advait.m.raut@gmail.com, upasana@cse.iitb.ac.in, bairi@cse.iitb.ac.in, ganesh@cse.iitb.ac.in

Abstract

Accelerated growth of the World Wide Web has resulted in the evolution of many online collaboration platforms in various domains, including education domain. These platforms, apart from bringing interested stakeholders together, also provide innovative and value added services such as smart search, notifications, suggestions, etc. Techpedia is one of such a platform which facilitates students to submit any original project description and aims to nurture the project idea by mentoring, collaborating and recognizing significant contributions by the system of awards and entrepreneurship. An important aspect of this platform is its ability to suggest a suitable mentor to a student's project. We propose an elegant approach to find an appropriate mentor for a given project by analyzing the project abstract. By analyzing past projects guided by various mentors and by engaging Wikipedia knowledge structure during the analysis, we show that our method suggests mentor(s) to a new project with good accuracy.

KEYWORDS: mentor suggestion, collaboration, information extraction, wikipedia.

1 Introduction

The internet has become more and more popular medium for online collaboration from past several years. Research suggests that collaborative learning has the potential to foster interaction and social support lacking in traditional learning environments [3]. Now a days online collaboration has pervaded into almost every field. There are varieties of platforms where people can collaborate and share their ideas, resources, techniques and work towards a common goal. The success of online collaboration has attracted more and more people/organizations to participate and grow the network. As the size of collaboration network increases, it poses many challenges in terms of resource management, organization, timely access to right piece of information, to name a few. This calls for sophisticated techniques and algorithms for better management and utilization of resources in a collaboration. In this paper we propose a solution to one of such problem (more precisely mentor identification problem, discussed later) in an academic domain. More specifically, we conducted our experiments on a well known collaboration platform called Techpedia [1]. However, we strongly believe that our techniques can be well adopted for any other academic collaboration platforms which support basic characteristics of an academic project life cycle management.

Techpedia is one of well known online collaborative platform for technology projects by students to link the needs of industry and grassroots innovators with young minds and to promote collaborative research. It facilitates students and innovators to share their ideas/project and collaborate with mentors/guides, industries and sponsors. Every project will have one or more mentors who are competent in the project field and guide the project. As the number of projects and mentor network increases in size, it becomes very challenging for a person to identify and approach a mentor for his/her project manually. Hence it is important to have robust algorithms to automatically detect suitable mentors for a given project abstract.

Apart from providing collaboration platform, Techpedia also acts as a huge repository of past projects details such as abstracts, techniques, applications of projects, development details, mentor details, project related communication details, and many more. It also provides details about mentors such as their area of expertise, skill set, experience etc. By utilizing all these information, we propose an information extraction technique for mentor identification for a new project by analyzing its abstract.

Since project abstracts are generally very concise, we observed that augmenting the abstracts with related Wikipedia entities before running the extraction process produces a better result. In section 3 we empirically show that, this technique significantly improves our mentor suggestion accuracy.

Rest of the paper is organized as follows. In section 2 we state our problem more formally and provide solutions for mentor suggestion, in section 3 we compare the techniques that we proposed, in section 4 we provide the details of prior work and we end the paper with conclusion in section 5.

2 Mentor suggestion

2.1 Problem Definition

Given a set of past projects $\mathbb{P} = \left\{p_1, p_2, ...p_{|\mathbb{P}|}\right\}$, a pool of mentors $\mathbb{M} = \left\{m_1, m_2, ...m_{|\mathbb{M}|}\right\}$, and a set of catalogs (like Wikipedia, Wikipedia Miner, etc) $\mathbb{W} = \left\{W_1, W_2, ...W_{|\mathbb{W}|}\right\}$, we would like to determine a subset $M \subseteq \mathbb{M}$ of mentors who can best guide a new project p.

Each project p_i has a set of attributes like owner, title, abstract, description, mentors who guided the project, inception date, duration, students who worked on them, sponsors, etc. We refer these attributes using dot notation as shown below: $p_i.title =< project\ title >$; $p_i.abstract =< project\ abstract >$; $p_i.mentors = \left\{set\ of\ mentors\ guided\ project\ p_i\right\}$

Similarly, each mentor has attributes like name, id, organization, work experience, a brief technical profile explaining his/her skill area and technical competence, etc. Again, as in case of projects, we represent these attributes using dot notation.

Formally, we define the problem as learning a function θ that suggests the mentors for the project p as follows:

$$\theta = \left\{M \mid p, \mathbb{P}, \mathbb{M}, \mathbb{W}\right\}$$

2.2 The Algorithm

We addressed our problem using two different approaches and compared the results. In sections 2.2.1, 2.2.2 we describe our approaches, which we compare and evaluate in section 3.

2.2.1 VSM over Past Project

In this approach, we tokenized the abstracts of each project in $\mathbb{P} = \left\{p_1, p_2, ...p_{|\mathbb{P}|}\right\}$, and represented each project in a Vector Space Model (VSM), after removing stop words and stemming. Using jaccard and cosine similarity measures we found out similarity between the target project p and the past projects $\mathbb{P}$. The mentors of the best matched past project are suggested as the mentors for the new project p. The Algorithm 1 outlines this approach.

Algorithm 1 VSM over Past Project

input: New project p, Past projects $\mathbb{P}$, Mentor pool $\mathbb{M}$
output: Suggested mentors $M \subseteq \mathbb{M}$
Initialize $M = \{\varnothing\}$, $p_{best} = \varnothing$, $V_{best} = \varnothing$
V_p =Vector Space Model of $p.abstract$
▷ Find best matching project
for $i = 1$ to $|\mathbb{P}|$ **do**
  V_i =Vector Space Model of p_i
  if $CosineSimilarity\left(V_p, V_i\right) > CosineSimilarity\left(V_p, V_{best}\right)$ **then**
    $p_{best} = p_i$
    $V_{best} = V_i$
  end if
end for
$M = p_{best}.mentors$ /Comment Mentors of p_{best}
  return M

2.2.2 VSM over Combination of Wikipedia Entities and Project Abstracts

In general, the project abstracts are short and concise. Due to this, the vector representation of these abstracts in VSM becomes highly sparse. This leads to poor jaccard and cosine similarities in approaches presented in section 2.2.1. To alleviate this problem, we propose a technique called Wikification. The following are the steps of Wikification:

1. Entity Spotting: We spot Wikipedia entities in every project abstract using Wikipedia Miner.
2. Entity Disambiguation: In some cases, multiple Wikipedia entities can match for a spotted word or phrase. In such cases, we disambiguate the entities based on the context available in the project abstract.
3. Semantic Expansion: For each of the identified entities in previous two steps, we collect semantically related entities by exploiting Wikipedia structure. Wikipedia maintains various kinds relations between the entities through hyperlinks, categories, see also links, redirect pages, disambiguation pages, etc. We found three types of semantic relations suitable for our work. Table 1 explains these relations. As part of offline processing, these relations were extracted for every Wikipedia entity, indexed and stored in a repository. We made use of this repository for extracting required semantic relations.

Semantic relations	**Semantic values from Wikipedia page excerpts**
Synonym : Is instrumental in identifying entities which are known with different names.	All redirected names of the Wikipedia page and the values of the Info box attributes like 'Nick Name', 'Other Names' are stored under this class.Ex: For *Sony: Sony Corp, Sony Entertainment*
Association : An association signifies the connection between two query terms. It can be unidirectional where one entity includes other within its description. It can also be bidirectional i.e entities use each other in their description. Ex:For *Sony:Sony Ericsson, Sony Products*	All valid hyperlinks of a Wikipedia page.
Sibling : The entities which have one or more common parents	Siblings are the sub categories/ pages which do not follow hyponym pattern. Ex: For *Sony: list of sony trademarks*

Table 1: Semantic Relations extracted from Wikipedia

At the end of Wikification process, we get a set of Wikipedia entities that are related to the project abstracts. We used entity descriptions along with project abstract text to build a VSM. Using jaccard and cosine similarity measures we found out the similarity between the target project p and the expanded abstracts of past projects $\mathbb{P}$. The mentors of the best matched past project are suggested as the mentors for the new project p. The Algorithm 2 outlines this approach.

3 Experiments and Evaluation

3.1 Experimental Setup

Experiments and Evaluation was done on Techpedia corpus. We identified 600 projects and 64 associated mentors as our training and testing data. We manually inspected and corrected some of the projects where mentor assignment was not proper and some mentor profiles where data was missing.

Algorithm 2 VSM over Combination of Wikipedia Entities and Project Abstracts

```
input: New project p, Past projects ℙ, Mentor pool 𝕄, Catalogs 𝕎
output: Suggested mentors M ⊆ 𝕄
Initialize M = {∅}, p_best = ∅, V_best = ∅
                                          ▷ Find best matching project
for i = 1 to |ℙ| do
    V_i = Vector Space Model of p_i
                          ▷ Spot Wikipedia entities using Wikipedia Miner
    S = {Entities spotted in p_i.abstract by Wikipedia Miner}
    E = {∅}
    for each entity e ∈ S do
        E = E ∪ {Semantically related entities to e}
    end for
    p_i.expandedAbstract = p_i.abstract
    for each entity e ∈ E do
        p_i.expandedAbstract = p_i.expandedAbstract ∪ e.text
    end for
    V_p = Vector Space Model of p.expandedAbstract
    if CosineSimilarity(V_p, V_i) > CosineSimilarity(V_p, V_best) then
        p_best = p_i
        V_best = V_i
    end if
end for
M = p_best.mentors                                   ▷ Mentors of p_best
    return M
```

We used Wikipedia Miner APIs to query and extract spotting details from Wikipedia Miner portal services. We also used offline Wikipedia dump (2011) and extracted semantic relations (detailed in Table 1) of all Wikipedia entities offline, indexed and stored them them using Lucene for quicker access and processing.

3.2 Evaluation Methodology

We adopted 2 fold evaluation methodology where we split our data (600 projects) into training and testing sets. We loosely use the word training here to refer the set of past projects from which we learn the mentor-project relationship. We treated the projects in testing set as new projects by masking the mentors assigned to those projects. We then evaluate the accuracy of our system by comparing the suggested mentors to the masked mentors. We propose two schemes of evaluation: 1. Coarse Grained Evaluation, 2. Fine Grained Evaluation.

3.2.1 Coarse Grained Evaluation

For each project in Test set, ranked mentor list was found based on the similarity score of matching test project abstract with the past project abstracts from the training set. For evaluation, we considered mentor is correctly identified if the actual mentor (which was masked before running the test) is present in top-k mentors of the ranked mentor list. We evaluated our system for k=5, 10 and 15. Figures 1a, 1b, 1c show the result of coarse grained evaluation.

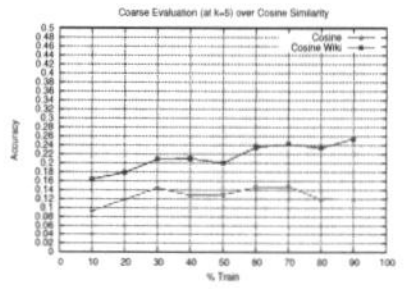

(a) Precision @ 5

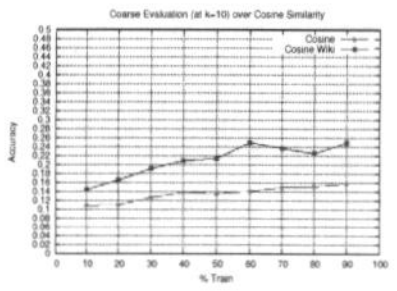

(b) Precision @10

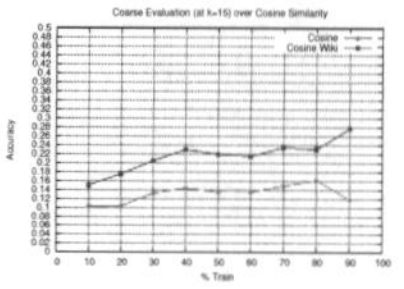

(c) Precision @15

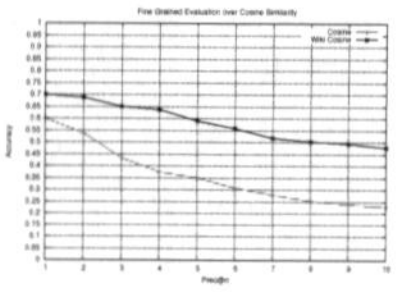

(d) Fine grained

Figure 1: Evaluation Results

3.2.2 Fine Grained Evaluation

Note that, there can be multiple mentors for the same field of work. It is acceptable to have any one of those mentors as the suggested mentor by the system. But our previous scheme of evaluation (section 3.2.1) does not consider this, resulting in poor accuracy. Hence we devised a new evaluation scheme (we call it Fine Grained Evaluation) wherein, we manually inspect if the system suggested mentors for the projects in test set fall under the same area of expertise as demanded by the projects. Since it was tedious to manually evaluate 600 projects, we randomly selected 100 projects which we further split into 60:40 as train and test sets. As in the previous scheme, here again we obtained a ranked list of mentors and evaluated precision at top-k. Figure 1d shows the result of fine grained evaluation.

3.3 Observations

3.3.1 Coarse Grained Evaluation

We observe that using Wikipedia Miner along with semantic expansion (Algorithm 2) has yielded better accuracies than rest of the methods(Algorithms 1).

3.3.2 Fine grained evaluation

Even with this scheme, we observe that using Wikipedia Miner along with semantic expansion (Algorithm 2) has yielded better accuracies than rest of the methods (Algorithms 1).

4 Prior Work

The work [4]describes two stage model for finding experts relevant to a user query: relevance and co-occurrence. Co-occurrence model learns co-occurrence between terms and the author of that document. [5] social search model aims to rank expert answerer to a user query by assigning topics to query using Latent Dirichlet Allocation [2]. Wikipedia Miner [6, 7] aims to find and link Wikipedia entities within a document with entity disambiguation.

5 Conclusion

We presented a body of techniques to suggest suitable mentors for a new submitted project in an online collaborative platform like Techpedia. Our work was hinged around the need of selecting a mentor for a project in a large corpus of projects with ease and accuracy. We demonstrated with multiple different techniques how this can be achieved. We also showed how an external catalog like Wikipedia can be engaged to enhance the accuracy of suggestion and empirically proved that semantic expansion yields better results. As part of our future work, we aim to improve the accuracy of suggestion by considering mentor's technical profile more rigorously and by adopting semantic analysis of project details using NLP techniques.

References

[1] http://www.techpedia.in.

[2] David M. Blei, Andrew Y. Ng, and Michael I. Jordan. Latent dirichlet allocation. *J. Mach. Learn. Res.*, 3:993–1022, March 2003.

[3] C. J. Bonk and K. S. King. Electronic collaborators: Learner-centered technologies for literacy, apprenticeship, and discourse. March 1998.

[4] [Y Cao et al. A two-stage model for expert search. MSR-TR-2008., 2008.

[5] Damon Horowitz and Sepandar D. Kamvar. The anatomy of a large-scale social search engine. In *Proceedings of the 19th international conference on World wide web*, WWW '10, pages 431–440, New York, NY, USA, 2010. ACM.

[6] Olena Medelyan, Ian H. Witten, and David Milne. Topic indexing with wikipedia.

[7] David Milne and Ian H. Witten. Learning to link with wikipedia. In *Proceedings of the 17th ACM conference on Information and knowledge management*, CIKM '08, pages 509–518, New York, NY, USA, 2008. ACM.

Automatically Assessing Free Texts

Yllias Chali   Sadid A. Hasan
University of Lethbridge, Lethbridge, AB, Canada
chali@cs.uleth.ca, hasan@cs.uleth.ca

ABSTRACT
Evaluation of the content of free texts is a challenging task for humans. Automation of this process is largely useful in order to reduce human related errors. We consider one instance of the "free texts" assessment problems; automatic essay grading where the task is to grade student written essays automatically given course materials and a set of human-graded essays as training data. We use a Latent Semantic Analysis (LSA)-based methodology to accomplish this task. We experiment on a dataset obtained from an occupational therapy course and report the results. We also discuss our findings, analyze different problem areas and explain the potential solutions.

KEYWORDS: Free texts, essay grading, latent semantic analysis, syntactic tree kernel, shallow semantic tree kernel.

1 Introduction

The problem of assessing free texts involves understanding the inner meaning of the free texts. Automation of free text assessment is necessary specially when an expert evaluator is unavailable in today's Internet-based learning environment. This is also useful to reduce human related errors such as "rater effects" (Rudner, 1992). Research to automate the assessment of free texts, such as grading student-written essays, has been carried out over the years. The earlier approaches such as Project Essay Grade (PEG) (Page and Petersen, 1995) and e-rater (Powers et al., 2000) were solely based on some simple surface features that took essay-length, number of commas etc. into consideration whereas recent research has tended to focus on understanding the inner meaning of the texts. Latent Semantic Analysis (LSA) (Landauer et al., 1998; Deerwester et al., 1990) has been shown to fit well in addressing this task previously (Kakkonen et al., 2006; Kakkonen and Sutinen, 2004; Briscoe et al., 2010). LSA uses a sophisticated approach to decode the inherent relationships between a context (typically a sentence, a paragraph or a document) and the words that they contain. The main idea behind the LSA is to measure the semantic similarities to be found between two texts from words contained within. In this paper, we use LSA to automatically grade student-written essays. We experiment with different local and global weighting functions[1]. Experiments on an occupational therapy dataset show that the performance of the LSA varies with respect to the weighting function used. In the next sections, we present an overview of LSA, describe our approach, and present the evaluation results. We then discuss various problem areas related to the evaluation framework and explain potential solutions. Finally, we conclude the paper.

2 Overview of LSA

LSA, that has been used successfully in various NLP tasks (Cederberg and Widdows, 2003; Clodfelder, 2003; Kanejiya et al., 2003; Pino and Eskenazi, 2009), can determine the similarity of the meaning of words and the context based on word co-occurrence information (Kakkonen et al., 2006). In the first phase of LSA, a word-by-context (WCM) matrix is constructed that represents the number of times each distinct word appears in each context. Next, weighting may be applied to the values contained in this matrix in relation to their frequency in order to better represent the importance of a word. The main idea of using a weighting function is to give higher values to the words that are more important for the content and lower values otherwise (Kakkonen and Sutinen, 2004). The next phase is called the dimensionality reduction step. In this phase, the dimension of the WCM is reduced by applying Singular Value Decomposition (SVD) and then reducing the number of singular values in SVD. This is done in order to try and draw out underlying latent semantic similarities between texts in the decomposition when comparison operators are used. This step also enables words that are used in a similar fashion, but not necessarily in the same documents, to be viewed as having a similar role (synonymy) in the texts, thus, enhancing their similarity scores. By reducing the dimensions, LSA can enhance the score of two similar documents whilst decreasing the score of non similar documents. Thus the process makes the context and the words more dependent to each other by reducing the inherent noise of the data set (Jorge-Botana et al., 2010).

3 Our Approach

Our approach is most closely related to the approach described in Kakkonen and Sutinen (2004) where the experiments were conducted in the Finnish language. However, in this work, we

[1] An estimation to calculate the representativeness of a word in a document.

experiment with the essays and course materials written in the English language. The main idea is based on the assumption that a student's knowledge is largely dependent on learning the course content; therefore, the student's knowledge can be computed as the degree of semantic similarity between the essay and the given course materials. An essay will get a higher grade if it closely matches with the course content. The grading process includes three major steps. In the first step, we build a semantic space from the given course materials by constructing a word-by-context matrix (WCM). Here we use different local and global weighting functions to build several LSA models. In the next step, a set of pre-scored (human-graded) essays are transformed into a query-vector form similar to each vector in the WCM and then their similarity with the semantic space is computed in order to define the threshold values for each grade category. The similarity score for each essay is calculated by using the traditional cosine similarity measure. In the last step, the student-written to-be-graded essays are transformed into the query-vector forms and compared to the semantic space in a similar way. The threshold values for the grade categories are examined to specify which essay belongs to which grade category.

4 Experiments and Evaluation

4.1 System Description

Inspired by the work of Jorge-Botana et al. (2010), we experiment with different local and global weighting functions applied to the WCM. The main idea is to transform the raw frequency cell x_{ij} of the WCM into the product of a local term weight l_{ij}, and a global term weight g_j. Given the term/document frequency matrix (WCM), a weighting algorithm is applied to each entry that has three components to makeup the new weighted value in the term/document matrix. This looks as: $w_{ij} = l_{ij} * g_j * N_j$, where w_{ij} is the weighted value for the ith term in the jth context, l_{ij} is the local weight for term i in the context j, g_j is the global weight for the term i across all contexts in the collection, and N_j is the normalization factor for context j.

Local Weighting: We use two local weighting methods in this work: *1) Logarithmic:* $\log\left(1 + f_{ij}\right)$, and *2) Term Frequency (TF):* f_{ij}, where f_{ij} is the number of times (frequency) the term i appears in the context j.

Global Weighting: We experiment with three global weighting methods: *1) Entropy:* $1 + \left(\frac{\sum_j (p_{ij} \log(p_{ij}))}{\log(n)}\right)$, *2) Inverse Document Frequency (IDF):* $\log\left(\frac{n}{df_i}\right) + 1$, and *3) Global Frequency/Inverse Document Frequency (GF/IDF):* $\frac{\sum_j f_{ij}}{df_i}$, where $p_{ij} = \frac{f_{ij}}{\sum_j f_{ij}}$, n is the number of documents in our word by context matrix, and df_i is the number of contexts in which the term i is present.

Different Models: By combining the different local and global weighting schemes, we build the following six different LSA models: **1) LE:** logarithmic local weighting and entropy-based global weighting, **2) LI:** logarithmic local weighting and IDF-based global weighting, **3) LG:** logarithmic local weighting and GF/IDF-based global weighting, **4) TE:** TF-based local weighting and entropy-based global weighting, **5) TI:** TF-based local weighting and IDF-based global weighting, and **6) TG:** TF-based local weighting and GF/IDF-based global weighting.

4.2 Implementation

We use a dataset obtained from an occupational therapy course where 3 journal articles are provided as the course materials. The students are asked to answer an essay-type question. The dataset contains 91 student-written essays, which are graded by a professor[2]. The length of the essays varied from 180 to 775 characters. For our experiments, we randomly choose 61 pre-scored essays to build the threshold values for different grade categories, and the rest of the essays are used as the test data. Initially, we split the course materials into 64 paragraphs and built the word-by-paragraph matrix by treating the paragraphs as contexts. Our preliminary experiments suggested that this scheme shows worse performance than that of using individual sentences as the contexts. So, we tokenized the course materials (journal articles) into 741 sentences and built the word-by-sentence matrix. We do not perform word stemming for our experiments. We use a stop word list of 429 words to remove any occurrence of them from the datasets. In this work, C++ and Perl are used as the programming languages to implement the LSA models. The GNU Scientific Library (GSL[3]) software package is used to perform the SVD calculations. During the dimensionality reduction step, we have experimented with different dimensions of the semantic space. Finally, we kept 100 as the number of dimensions since we got better results using this value.

4.3 Results and Discussion

In Table 1, we present the results of our experiments. The first column stands for the weighting model used ("N" denotes no weighting method applied, which acts as a baseline for this work). The "Correlation" column presents the Spearman rank correlation between the scores given by the professor and the systems. The "Accuracy" column stands for the proportion of the cases where the professor and the system have assigned the same grade whereas the next column shows the percentage of essays where the system-assigned grade is at most one point away or exactly the same as the professor. From these results, we can see that the performance of the systems varied (having correlation from 0.32 to 0.68) with respect to the weighting scheme applied. We see that the combination of the logarithmic local weighting with the entropy-based global weighting scheme performs the best for our dataset. However, the reason behind lower correlations of all the LSA models might be that the threshold values for the grade categories became largely dependent on the training essays and the course materials. This is because the grades were not evenly distributed among the given human-graded corpus (see Table 2). Ideally it is desirable to have the representative training essays across the spectrum of possible grades to set the thresholds on by using the SVD generated from the training materials. We believe that the use of a larger dataset while defining the thresholds might improve the LSA model's performance. The length of the essays is another issue since longer essays tend to capture more information in their representative vectors which provides the scope for a better similarity matching with the semantic space.

Weighting Model	Correlation	Accurate (%)	Accurate or one point away (%)
LE	0.68	40.2	73.1
LI	0.49	27.1	51.8
LG	0.40	21.3	42.2
TE	0.34	19.2	36.4
TI	0.52	32.6	58.6
TG	0.38	20.4	38.9
N	0.32	17.8	32.9

Table 1: Results

[2]Each essay is graded on a scale from 0 to 6.

[3]http://www.gnu.org/software/gsl/

Grade	Distribution (%)
0	1.10
1	1.10
2	1.10
3	12.08
4	25.27
5	24.17
6	35.16

Table 2: Grade distribution

5 Analyses and Solutions

5.1 Automating the Evaluation

The performance of the LSA models can be verified by measuring their correlation with the human-graded essays (as shown in Section 4.3). To omit the human intervention associated with this method, we can introduce an automatic evaluation module that uses syntactic and/or shallow semantic tree kernels to measure the textual similarity between the student-written essays and the given course materials. The basic LSA model that uses cosine similarity measure has one problem in automatic grading of academic essays. In this method, a student essay can obtain a good grade by having a very small number of highly representative terms that correlates the golden essays. This also means that the repetition of important terms without having any syntactic/semantic appropriateness can lead to a overstated grade (Jorge-Botana et al., 2010). So, we can check the LSA model's performance by measuring syntactic/semantic similarity of the student-written essays corresponding to the course materials. Syntactic and semantic features have been used successfully in various NLP tasks (Zhang and Lee, 2003; Moschitti et al., 2007; Moschitti and Basili, 2006). Based on some preliminary case-by-case analysis, we find the automatic evaluation model to be promising.

Syntactic Tree Kernel: Given the sentences, we can first parse them into syntactic trees using a parser like (Charniak, 1999) and then, calculate the similarity between the two trees using the *tree kernel* (Collins and Duffy, 2001). Once we build the trees (syntactic or semantic), our next task is to measure the similarity between the trees. For this, every tree T is represented by an m dimensional vector $v(T) = \big(v_1(T), v_2(T), \cdots v_m(T)\big)$, where the i-th element $v_i(T)$ is the number of occurrences of the i-th tree fragment in tree T. The tree kernel of two trees T_1 and T_2 is actually the inner product of $v(T_1)$ and $v(T_2)$: $TK(T_1, T_2) = v(T_1).v(T_2)$. TK is the similarity value (tree kernel) between a pair of sentences based on their syntactic structure.

Shallow Semantic Tree Kernel (SSTK): To calculate the semantic similarity between two sentences, we first parse the corresponding sentences semantically using the Semantic Role Labeling (SRL) (Moschitti et al., 2007; Kingsbury and Palmer, 2002; Hacioglu et al., 2003) system, ASSERT[4]. We represent the annotated sentences using tree structures called semantic trees (ST). The similarity between the two STs is computed using the shallow semantic tree kernel (SSTK) (Moschitti et al., 2007). This is the semantic similarity score between a pair of sentences based on their semantic structures.

5.2 Automating Data Generation

To experiment with the LSA-based model we require a number of student-written essays. It is often hard to collect a huge number of raw student-written essays and process them into

[4]Available at http://cemantix.org/assert

Essays (Score 6)	Example
Automatic	Since it seemed unlikely that Hans will be able to completely return to his former life structure, the following goals were established for his habituation: To modify Hans' habit patterns (i.e., identify new leisure activities to build into his schedule, especially on the weekend.), To enable Hans to acquire a new role (i.e., the role of a volunteer), To assist Hans to modify some of his roles (e.g., being a spectator or counselor, rather than a coach or participant during volley ball games), To establish a profile of Hans' work capacities through vocational testing and to secure appropriate vocational training and experience to enable return to a worker role.
Golden	Woodworking means a lot to Hans. He enjoys working with wood to build furniture and it is a goal he wants to achieve once again. He has the desire to regain the role of woodworker for a productivity as well. With modifications and techniques it can be achieved. Hans values this role and even after going to vocational testing he did not want to be an accountant. Woodworking goals would allow us to develop self efficacy in Hans as well as giving him a means for productivity to be independent once again. This will increase his self confidence and give back a habit.

Table 3: Example of an automatically generated essay and an original student-written essay

the machine-readable format. To reduce the human intervention involved in producing a large amount of training data, we could automate this process by using the ROUGE (Lin, 2004) toolkit. *ROUGE* stands for "Recall-Oriented Understudy for Gisting Evaluation". It is a collection of measures that count the number of overlapping units such as n-gram, word-sequences, and word-pairs between the system-generated summary to be evaluated and the ideal summaries created by humans. We can apply ROUGE to automatically generate extract-based essays given course materials and a set of golden (written by expert human) essays. We can assume each individual sentence of the course material as the candidate extract sentence and calculate its ROUGE similarity scores with the corresponding golden essay. Thus an average ROUGE score is assigned to each sentence in the document. We can choose the top N sentences based on ROUGE scores to have the label $+1$ (candidate essay sentences) and the rest to have the label -1 (non-essay sentences) and thus, we can generate essays up to a predefined word limit considering different levels of expertise of the students. In our preliminary experiments, we have generated 214 essays from the given course materials. We have used 20 golden essays[5] in this experiment. The automatically generated essays appeared to be similar in content to that of the original student-written essays. We show an example in Table 3.

Conclusion and Future Work

We used LSA to automatically grade student-written essays. We experimented with different local and global weighting functions applied to the word-by-context matrix. Our experiments revealed that the performance of the LSA model varies with the use of different weighting functions. We also discussed our solutions to reduce human intervention by automating the evaluation framework and the data generation process. In future, we plan to perform large-scale experiments on some other datasets with longer essays and examine how the LSA model's performance varies with respect to different weighting methods.

Acknowledgments

The research reported in this paper was supported by the MITACS Accelerate internship program, the Natural Sciences and Engineering Research Council (NSERC) of Canada – discovery grant and the University of Lethbridge. The authors gratefully acknowledge the assistance provided by Dr. Colin Layfield and Dr. Laurence Meadows.

[5]We treated the essays that got the full score of 6 as the golden essays.

References

Briscoe, T., Medlock, B., and Andersen, O. (2010). Automated Assessment of ESOL Free Text Examinations. In *Technical Report UCAM-CL-TR-790 ISSN 1476-2986*, University of Cambridge.

Cederberg, S. and Widdows, D. (2003). Using lsa and noun coordination information to improve the precision and recall of automatic hyponymy extraction. In *Proceedings of the seventh conference on Natural language learning at HLT-NAACL 2003 - Volume 4*, pages 111–118. ACL.

Charniak, E. (1999). A Maximum-Entropy-Inspired Parser. In *Technical Report CS-99-12*, Brown University, Computer Science Department.

Clodfelder, K. A. (2003). An lsa implementation against parallel texts in french and english. In *Proceedings of the HLT-NAACL 2003 Workshop on Building and using parallel texts: data driven machine translation and beyond - Volume 3*, pages 111–114. ACL.

Collins, M. and Duffy, N. (2001). Convolution Kernels for Natural Language. In *Proceedings of Neural Information Processing Systems*, pages 625–632, Vancouver, Canada.

Deerwester, S., Dumais, S., Furnas, G., Landauer, T., and Harshman, R. (1990). Indexing by Latent Semantic Analysis. *Journal of the American Society for Information Science*, 41(6):391–407.

Hacioglu, K., Pradhan, S., Ward, W., Martin, J. H., and Jurafsky, D. (2003). Shallow Semantic Parsing Using Support Vector Machines. In *Technical Report TR-CSLR-2003-03*, University of Colorado.

Jorge-Botana, G., Leon, J. A., Olmos, R., and Escudero, I. (2010). Latent Semantic Analysis Parameters for Essay Evaluation using Small-Scale Corpora. *Journal of Quantitative Linguistics*, 17(1):1–29.

Kakkonen, T., Myller, N., and Sutinen, E. (2006). Applying Part-Of-Speech Enhanced LSA to Automatic Essay Grading. In *Proceedings of the 4th IEEE International Conference on Information Technology: Research and Education (ITRE 2006)*.

Kakkonen, T. and Sutinen, E. (2004). Automatic Assessment of the Content of Essays Based on Course Materials. In *Proceedings of the 2nd IEEE International Conference on Information Technology: Research and Education*, pages 126–130.

Kanejiya, D., Kumar, A., and Prasad, S. (2003). Automatic evaluation of students' answers using syntactically enhanced lsa. In *Proceedings of the HLT-NAACL 03 workshop on Building educational applications using natural language processing - Volume 2*, pages 53–60. ACL.

Kingsbury, P. and Palmer, M. (2002). From Treebank to PropBank. In *Proceedings of the International Conference on Language Resources and Evaluation*, Las Palmas, Spain.

Landauer, T., Foltz, P., and Laham, D. (1998). An Introduction to Latent Semantic Analysis. *Discourse Processes*, 25(2):259–284.

Lin, C. (2004). ROUGE: A Package for Automatic Evaluation of Summaries. In *Proceedings of Workshop on Text Summarization Branches Out, Post-Conference Workshop of Association for Computational Linguistics*, pages 74–81, Barcelona, Spain.

Moschitti, A. and Basili, R. (2006). A Tree Kernel Approach to Question and Answer Classification in Question Answering Systems. In *Proceedings of the 5th International Conference on Language Resources and Evaluation*, Genoa, Italy.

Moschitti, A., Quarteroni, S., Basili, R., and Manandhar, S. (2007). Exploiting Syntactic and Shallow Semantic Kernels for Question/Answer Classificaion. In *Proceedings of the 45th Annual Meeting of the Association of Computational Linguistics (ACL 2007)*, pages 776–783, Prague, Czech Republic.

Page, E. B. and Petersen, N. S. (1995). The Computer Moves into Essay Grading: Updating the Ancient Test. *Phi Delta Kappan*, 76(7).

Pino, J. and Eskenazi, M. (2009). An application of latent semantic analysis to word sense discrimination for words with related and unrelated meanings. In *Proceedings of the Fourth Workshop on Innovative Use of NLP for Building Educational Applications*, pages 43–46. ACL.

Powers, D. E., Burstein, J., Chodorow, M., Fowles, M. E., and Kukich, K. (2000). Comparing the validity of automated and human essay scoring. *(GRE No. 98-08a, ETS RR-00-10). Princeton, NJ: Educational Testing Service.*

Rudner, L. M. (1992). Reducing Errors Due to the Use of Judges. *Practical Assessment, Research & Evaluation*, 3(3).

Zhang, A. and Lee, W. (2003). Question Classification Using Support Vector Machines. In *Proceedings of the Special Interest Group on Information Retrieval*, pages 26–32, Toronto, Canada. ACM.

Automatic pronunciation assessment for language learners with acoustic-phonetic features

Vaishali Patil, Preeti Rao
Department of Electrical Engineering,
Indian Institute of Technology Bombay,
Mumbai, India.
{vvpatil, prao}@ee.iitb.ac.in

ABSTRACT

Computer-aided spoken language learning has been an important area of research. The assessment of a learner's pronunciation with respect to native pronunciation lends itself to automation using speech recognition technology. However phone recognition accuracies achievable in state-of-the-art automatic speech recognition systems make their direct application challenging. In this work, linguistic knowledge and the knowledge of speech production are incorporated to obtain a system that discriminates clearly between native and non-native speech. Experimental results on aspirated consonants of Hindi by 10 speakers shows that acoustic-phonetic features outperform traditional cepstral features in a statistical likelihood based assessment of pronunciation.

KEYWORDS : acoustic-phonetic features, language learners, pronunciation, aspirated stops.

1 Introduction

Fluency in spoken language by a language learner must be judged based on the achieved articulation and prosody in comparison with that of native speakers of the language. The articulation is influenced by how well the learner has mastered the pronunciation of the phone set of the new language as well as the usage of the phones in the context of the words. Language learning is an important activity and automating aspects of it via speech recognition technology has been an area of recent research globally (Strik et al., 2007). One aspect of spoken language learning that lends itself to such automation is the assessment of pronunciation. The phones uttered by the speaker can be compared to their native acoustic forms to provide corrective feedback about the extent and type of errors. Automatic speech recognition (ASR) technology would seem to provide the solution to automatic pronunciation error detection by its ability to decode speech into word and phone sequences and provide acoustic likelihood scores indicating the match with trained native speech models. However, state-of-the-art ASR systems fare poorly on phone recognition accuracy unless aided by powerful language models. In an application such as pronunciation assessment, language models would obscure genuine pronunciation errors by the non-native learner. Further, for better raw phone recognition accuracy, the acoustic models need to be trained on actual non-native speech. Such a speech database is unlikely to be available.

A way to deal with the problem of poor phone recognition accuracies from ASR is to exploit any available knowledge about the type of pronunciation errors. It is observed, for instance, that the errors made by a non-native speaker learning the language (L2) tend to be heavily influenced by his own native tongue (L1). These phone segment level errors arise from (1) the absence of certain L2 phones in the L1 leading to phone substitutions by available similar phones, and (2) phonotactic constraints of L1 leading to improper usage of phones in certain word-level contexts. A knowledge of the common phone-level errors in the non-native speech can help to reduce the search space in speech decoding thus improving the phone recognition accuracy. However, since the phone errors typically involve phone substitution by closely matching phones borrowed from the speaker's L1, the discrimination is more challenging. Proper feature design in the acoustic space can contribute to improved discrimination between different phones that otherwise share several articulatory attributes. In the present work, we investigate the design of acoustic features in the context of specific pronunciation errors made by learners of spoken Hindi. We restrict ourselves to speakers whose L1 is Tamil. This language-pair provides prominent examples of phone substitution errors arising from the differences in the phonetic inventories of languages of two distinct language groups viz. Indo-Aryan (Hindi) and Dravidian (Tamil). Although the reported work is restricted to a specific type of pronunciation error, namely that relating to aspirated stops, the methodology presented in this paper can be usefully generalised.

In the next section, we describe the task of pronunciation assessment in the context of the chosen languages and the design of databases for training and system evaluation. Acoustic-phonetic features are described next followed by an experimental evaluation involving traditional ASR features as well.

2 Database design

The pronunciation assessment is carried out by specially constructed word lists that are read out by the language learner. The recorded utterances are processed by a speech recognition system to determine the pronunciation quality of each of the phones of interest with respect to native speech phone models. With our focus on Tamil learners of spoken Hindi, we should ideally have access to labelled data of Hindi speech from native Hindi speakers as well as from non-native (Tamil) speakers in order to build phone models for the automatic phone recognition system. However, a sizeable database of non-native speech is an unavailable resource. Linguistic knowledge about the phonetic inventories of the two languages can help to overcome this problem partially with the substitute phone models trained on more easily available native speech databases (Bhat et al., 2010).

In the present work, we investigate the pronunciation of consonants, in particular, the unvoiced stops of Hindi. The Tamil and Hindi phonetic inventories differ significantly in this category as seen in Table 1 (Thangarajan et al., 2008). Due to the absence of aspirated unvoiced stops in Tamil, learners of Hindi whose L1 is Tamil tend to substitute these phones with the closest available phone viz. the same place-of-articulation unvoiced unaspirated stop. Table 2 provides some example words with their observed pronunciations by native and non-native speakers. Assuming that the articulation of the unvoiced unaspirated stops is the same in both languages for a given place-of-articulation, we can use native Hindi speakers' speech for training the phone models for both native and non-native speakers. In the present work we use an available dataset of Marathi speech (another Indo-Aryan language that shares nearly all the phones of Hindi) as training data. The Marathi database comprises the word utterances from 20 speakers where the words cover all consonant-vowel (CV) occurrences in the language.

Stop categories / PoA	Hindi/Marathi		Tamil	
	Unaspirated	Aspirated	Unaspirated	Aspirated
Labial	p	p^h	p	-
Dental	t̪	t̪^{h}	t̪	-
Retroflex	ʈ	ʈ^h	ʈ	-
Velar	k	k^h	k	-

TABLE 1 – IPA chart showing difference in unvoiced stops of Hindi/Marathi and Tamil.

Word	Meaning	Articulation by native speaker	Articulation by non-native speaker
खामोशी	Silence	k^{h}AmoshI	kAmoshI
ठिकाना	Location	ʈ^{h}ikAnA	ʈikAnA
तारिका	Starlet	t̪ArikA	t̪ArikA
पेशा	Profession	peshA	peshA

TABLE 2 – Examples of unvoiced stops in word initial as articulated by native and non-native speakers

The test data comprises of recordings of Hindi words uttered by 5 native (3M and 2F) and 5 non-native (3M and 2F) Hindi speakers. The words list comprises each unvoiced stop consonant 'C' in word initial position with 8 words per consonant. These words are embedded in two Hindi sentences (one statement and one question form) acting as carrier phrases. The native speakers had good fluency in Hindi. In case of the non-native speakers (familiar with Hindi but not using it regularly), we focussed on Tamil L1speakers. They could read the Devnagiri script of Hindi having studied the language formally in school. The speakers were asked to go through the word list (Devnagiri spelling with English meaning) mentally before recording to ensure that they have no difficulty in reading. All recordings were made at 16 kHz sampling rate.

3 Proposed pronunciation assessment system

Given the recorded words from a test speaker, the system should quantify the "distance" of a realised phone from the canonical model of the intended phone. An overall measure of pronunciation quality can then be obtained by summarising the distances over the entire word list along with feedback on specific pronunciation errors. A widely used distance measure in pronunciation assessment is a normalized acoustic likelihood score obtained within a statistical speech recognition framework (Strik et al., 2007). The effectiveness of this measure depends on the acoustic features used to derive the observation vector. Standard HMM-based systems use MFCC features representing the spectral envelope of speech sounds. Such systems are known to confuse phones within the same broad manner classes and depend heavily on language modelling for acceptable speech recognition accuracy. On the other hand, research by speech scientists over the years has suggested that acoustic-phonetic cues obtained by the understanding of speech production can be usefully applied to discriminate phones that differ in a single attribute (Niyogi and Ramesh, 2003; Truong et al., 2004). In the next section, we present acoustic-phonetic features for discriminating aspiration in stop phones. These features are incorporated in a statistical phone recognition system. For comparison, a standard MFCC-based system is also implemented and evaluated on the same task. Both systems share a common first stage of broad-class segmentation (by aligning with the known transcription from the word list) with a 3-state diagonal covariance HMM-based system using the 39-dim MFCC vector (Young et al., 2006). The segmented unvoiced stops so obtained are used in pronunciation assessment of the aspiration attribute separately with each of two feature sets, viz. acoustic-phonetic and MFCC.

4 Acoustic-phonetic (AP) features for aspiration detection

The production of aspirated stops is similar to that of the same-place unaspirated stops but for the additional glottal aspiration that accompanies the onset of the following vowel. The main differentiating acoustic cues are either durational in terms of the longer voicing onset time (VOT) in the case of aspirated CV, or spectral, by way of the presence of cues associated with breathy voice quality. The features are presented next (Patil and Rao, 2011).

Frication duration: is the duration between the burst release and voicing onset. These landmarks are determined by refinement of the segment boundaries obtained in the HMM based broad class segmentation (Patil et al., 2009).

Difference between the first and second harmonic (H1-H2): is an indicator of breathiness since amplitude of the first harmonic relative to that of the second is proportional to the open quotient of glottis. It is computed from the short-time spectrum of a 25 ms window and averaged over 5 frames in the region 6 to 10 ms from the vowel onset.

Spectral tilt A1-A3: is the difference between the strongest spectral component in [100, 1000 Hz] and the one in [1800, 4000 Hz] thus capturing the difference of the energy between the first and third formant regions. Breathy voices are characterised by greater spectral tilt and hence greater A1-A3. It is computed by the same short-time spectrum averaging as used for H1-H2.

Signal-to-noise ratio: The superimposed aspiration leads to a lower harmonics-to-noise ratio in the vowel region immediately following an aspirated stop. This can be accurately estimated by a cepstrum based SNR computed over duration 25 ms starting 6 ms from the detected vowel onset.

B1-band energy: It is computed in the band of 400 Hz to 2000 Hz from the average power spectrum of vowel region using 25ms window for 5 frames every 1ms from vowel onset point. Lower values of this parameter characterize the presence of breathiness due to aspiration.

5 Experiments and results

The two systems using two different acoustic feature sets are used to obtain the statistical likelihood for the presence or absence of aspiration for each unvoiced stop across the entire list of word utterances by a test speaker. The MFCC-based system uses the HMM phone recogniser in a 2-class (aspirated/unaspirated) forced alignment mode on the unvoiced stops using 39 MFCCs. The AP system uses a 5-dimensional feature vector in a GMM framework.

A likelihood ratio distance measure is computed using equation (1) (Niyogi and Ramesh, 2003).

$$d(x)=\log\left(\frac{L(x\mid\wedge 1)}{L(x\mid\wedge 2)}\right) \tag{1}$$

where $L(x|\wedge 1)$ is the likelihood of a test point x in the observation space for model of class 1 (likewise $L(x|\wedge 2)$ for class 2). Here class1 refers to unaspirated stops and class2 to aspirated stops. In case of proper articulation, d(x) is expected to be greater than zero for unaspirated stops and less than zero for aspirated stops.

For each test speaker, we compute the distribution of the likelihood ratios computed across the speaker's set of *intended* unaspirated stops and also across the set of *intended* aspirated stops. If the stops are all properly articulated, we expect a good separation of the two distributions. Fig. 1 show the distributions obtained for each of the 10 native and non-native speakers using the AP features system. We note the prominent difference in the extent of overlap between the likelihood ratios in the case of native speakers with respect to that of non-native speakers. Fig. 2 shows the corresponding results for the MFCC feature system. While there is a difference in the overlap observed for the non-native speakers, the distinction between native and non-native speakers is much more clear across speakers with the AP features.

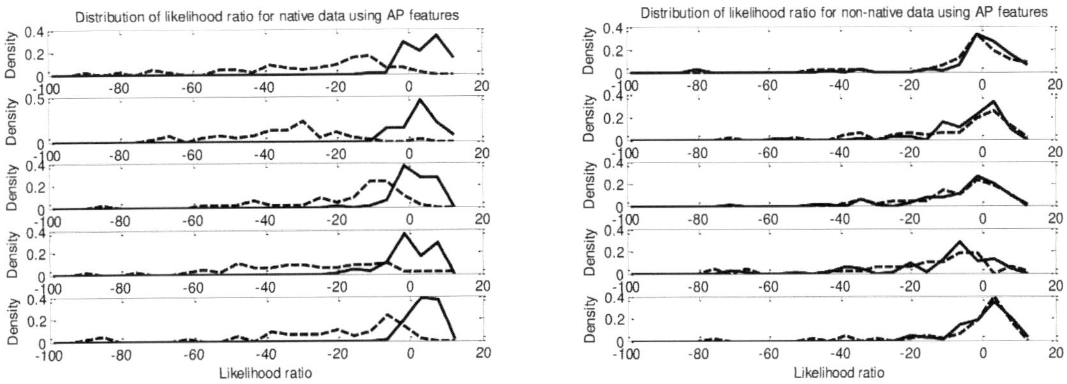

FIGURE 1 – Speaker wise distribution of likelihood ratio for native and non-native data using AP cues (solid line: intended unaspirated; dashed line: intended aspirated)

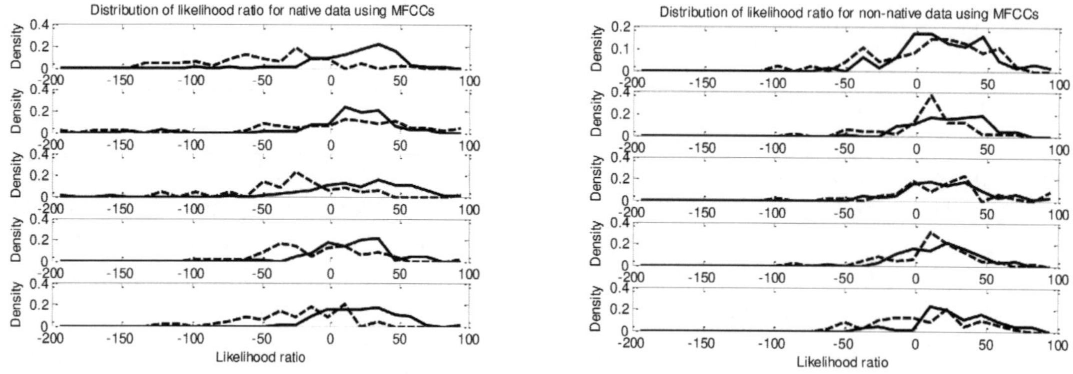

FIGURE 2 – Speaker wise distribution of likelihood ratio for native and non-native data using MFCCs (solid line: intended unaspirated; dashed line: intended aspirated)

Native test set			Non-native test set		
Speaker no.	AP	MFCCs	Speaker no.	AP	MFCCs
1	132.79	79.66	1	0.01	2.11
2	373.42	2.12	2	3.3	11.38
3	76.57	12.89	3	0.3	0.29
4	113.87	23.09	4	0.56	1.08
5	74.72	67.88	5	6.91	14.41

TABLE 3 – Speaker wise F-ratio of unaspirated-aspirated likelihood ratio for native and non-native test sets.

The difference between the performances of MFCC and AP features in the task of detecting non-native pronunciation can be understood from the values of F-ratios across the 10 speakers in Table 3. The F-ratio is computed for the pair of corresponding of unaspirated-aspirated likelihood ratio distributions for each speaker and each feature set. A larger value of F-ratio indicates a better separation of the particular speaker's aspirated and unaspirated utterances in the corresponding feature space, which may be interpreted as higher intelligibility. We see from Table 3 that this intelligibility measure takes on distinctly different values in the case of the AP feature based system, and consequently an accurate detection of non-nativeness is possible. In the case of the MFCC features, however, there is no clear threshold separating the F-ratios of non-native from native speakers.

To summarise, we have proposed a methodology for evaluating pronunciation quality in the context of a selected phonemic attribute. It was demonstrated that acoustic-phonetic features provide better discriminability between correctly and incorrectly uttered aspirated stops of Hindi compared with the more generic MFCC features. Future work will address other phonemic attributes while also expanding the dataset of test speakers.

References

Bhat, C., Srinivas, K. L. and Rao, P. (2010). Pronunciation scoring for language learners using a phone recognition system. *Proc. of the First International Conference on Intelligent Interactive Technologies and Multimedia 2010*, pages 135-139, Allahabad, India.

Niyogi, P. and Ramesh, P. (2003). The voicing feature for stop consonants: recognition experiments with continuously spoken alphabets. *Speech Communication*, 41: 349-367.

Patil, V., Joshi, S. and Rao, P. (2009). Improving the robustness of phonetic segmentation to accent and style variation with a two-staged approach. *Proc. of Interspeech 2009*, pages 2543-2546, Brighton, U.K.

Patil, V. and Rao, P. (2011). Acoustic features for detection of aspirated stops. *Proc. of National Conf. on Communication 2011*, pages 1-5, Bangalore, India.

Strik, H., Troung, K., Wet F. and Cucchiarini, C. (2007). Comparing classifiers for pronunciation error detection. *Proc. of Interspeech 2007*, pages 1837-1840, Antwerp, Belgium.

Thangarajan, R., Natarajan, A. and Selvam, M. (2008). Word and Triphone Based Approaches in Continuous Speech Recognition for Tamil Language. *WSEAS Transactions on Signal Processing*, 4(3): 76-86.

Truong, K., Neri, A., Cuchiarini, C. and Strik, H. (2004). Automatic pronunciation error detection: an acoustic-phonetic approach. *Proc. of the InSTIL/ICALL Symposium*, 2004, pages 135–138, Venice, Italy.

Young, S. et al. (2006). The HTK Book v3.4. Cambridge University.

An Issue-oriented Syllabus Retrieval System based on Terminology-based Syllabus Structuring and Visualization

Hideki Mima[1]

(1) School of Engineering, University of Tokyo, Hongo 7-3-1, Bunkyo-ku, Tokyo 113-0033, Japan

mima@t-adm.t.u-tokyo.ac.jp n

ABSTRACT

The purpose of this research was to develop an issue-oriented syllabus retrieval system that combined terminological processing, information retrieval, similarity calculation-based document clustering, and visualization.

Recently, scientific knowledge has grown explosively because of rapid advancements that have occurred in academia and society. Because of this dramatic expansion of knowledge, learners and educators sometimes struggle to comprehend the overall aspects of syllabi. In addition, learners may find it difficult to discover appropriate courses of study from syllabi because of the increasing growth of interdisciplinary studies programs. We believe that an issue-oriented syllabus structure might be more efficient because it provides clear directions for users. In this paper, we introduce an issue-oriented automatic syllabus retrieval system that integrates automatic term recognition as an issue extraction, and similarity calculation as terminology-based document clustering. We use automatically-recognized terms to represent each lecture in clustering and visualization. Retrieved syllabi are automatically classified based on their included terms or issues. The main goal of syllabus retrieval and classification is the development of an issue-oriented syllabus retrieval website that will present users with distilled knowledge in a concise form. In comparison with conventional systems, simple keyword-based syllabus retrieval is based on the assumption that our methods can provide users, and, in particular, novice users (students), with efficient lecture retrieval from an enormous number of syllabi. The system is currently in practical use for issue-oriented syllabus retrieval and clustering for syllabi for the University of Tokyo's Open Course Ware and for the School/Department of Engineering. Usability evaluations based on questionnaires used to survey over 100 students revealed that our proposed system is sufficiently efficient at syllabus retrieval.

KEYWORDS: Issue oriented, syllabus retrieval, term extraction, knowledge structuring, visualization

---

1 Introduction

Recently, scientific knowledge has grown explosively because of rapid advancements that have occurred in academia and society.[1] This rapid expansion of knowledge has made it increasingly difficult for learners and educators to comprehend the overall aspects of syllabi. In addition, because of the rapid growth of interdisciplinary studies programs, such as energy studies and earth-environmental studies, learners have found it increasingly difficult to discover appropriate courses of study in their syllabi.

Syllabus retrieval is believed to be one of several solutions to these problems. In fact, several syllabus retrieval systems have been proposed. In general, current syllabus retrieval methods can be classified as query-oriented and/or issue-oriented. Although the query-oriented method is useful and possesses strong retrieval capabilities, it can be difficult to employ, especially for novices, because the generation of queries usually requires users to first clarify their subjects.

The issue-oriented syllabus retrieval method was developed in an attempt to provide clear directions to learners. The issue-oriented syllabus structure is believed to be more efficient for learning and education, because it requires less knowledge about subjects (Mima et al., 2006). However, this system generally requires that users classify all syllabi manually in advance. This can be a time-consuming task. Thus, we can see that it is important to develop a more efficient method for automatic syllabus structuring to accelerate syllabus classification. The advantage of this technique is based on the assumption that automatic methods will enable more efficient processing of enormous amounts of syllabi texts.

In this paper, we introduce an innovative issue-oriented automatic syllabus classification system. We integrate automatic term recognition as issue extraction, terminology-based similarity-calculation for clustering, information retrieval, and visualization. Automatically-recognized terms are used to represent each lecture (or class) in clustering. In the system, provided syllabi are automatically classified and labeled according to the included terms that were automatically extracted. The main goal of syllabus retrieval and clustering is to develop an issue-oriented syllabus retrieval website that will present distilled knowledge to users in a concise form. The advantage of this system, in comparison with conventional syllabus retrieval or classification, is based on the assumption that automatic methods can efficiently process enormous amounts of text. The system has already been put into practical use for syllabus retrieval and clustering for the University of Tokyo's Open Course Ware and for the School/Department of Engineering syllabi. Usability evaluations based on questionnaires used to survey over 100 students revealed that our proposed system is sufficiently efficient at syllabus retrieval.

In the following section of this paper, we briefly explain the process of issue-oriented syllabi retrieval. We also provide an overview of the clustering system. In Section 2, we describe our proposed syllabus retrieval and classification scheme that is based on the use of automatically-extracted terms and on a visualization technique. In Sections 3 and 4, we discuss terminological processing as a feature extraction from each syllabus for similarity calculation and

1 For example, the Medline database (http://www.ncbi.nlm.nih.gov/pubmed) currently contains over 16 million paper abstracts in the domains of molecular biology, biomedicine, and medicine. The database is growing at a rate of more than 40,000 abstracts each month.

visualization. In Section 5, we present our evaluations of data collected from questionnaires used to survey over 100 students. We relied on the collected data to analyze the usability of our proposed scheme and to confirm its feasibility and efficiency. In the final Section, we present a summary of our approach and our conclusions.

2 System Overview

The main purpose of this study was to develop an efficient issue-oriented syllabus retrieval system that would provide clear directions to learners. Our approach to this issue-oriented syllabus classification system is based on the following:

- automatic term recognition (ATR) for automatic issue extraction
- automatic term clustering (ATC) for term variation management
- terminology-based document similarity calculation to develop syllabus classification
- automatic class label inference to clarify general issues of the classes

The system architecture is modular. It integrates the following components (see, Figure 1):

- *Terminology-based issue extraction (TIE)* – A component that conducts automatic term recognition as issue extraction from syllabus texts. It includes term extraction and term variation management.
- *Syllabus retriever (SR)* – It retrieves syllabi based on selected issues that are automatically extracted by TIE. It calculates similarities between each issue and each retrieved syllabus. Currently, we have adopted tf*idf based similarity calculation.
- *Similarity Calculation Engine(s) (SCE)* – It calculates similarities between KSs provided from each KR component by the use of ontology developed by ODE to show semantic similarities between each KSs. We adopted Vector Space Model-based (VSM) similarity calculation and we used terms as features of VSM. Semantic clusters of KSs were also provided.
- *SVM-based learning (SBL)* – A component that learns how to classify syllabi by extraction of classification patterns from features that have also been extracted by TFE. It then produces classification knowledge.
- *Terminology-based syllabus classification (SBC)* – It calculates similarities between syllabi provided by the SR component by the use of terms provided from TIE to develop clusters of syllabi. We adopted Vector Space Model-based (VSM) similarity calculation.
- *Term-based label inference (TLI)* – It infers representing labels for each class developed by TSC. We currently inferred labels based on term frequency (tf) for importance and document frequency (df) for generality.
- *Syllabus class visualizer (SCV)* – It visualizes syllabi structures based on graph expression in which classes of syllabi and representing labels of classes inferred by (TLI) are automatically provided.

As shown in Figure 1 and the flows by numbers, the system extracts issues automatically from syllabi texts in advance and produces classification of lectures based on these terms or issues. Then, representing labels (i.e., class labels) are also inferred by the use of terminological information. Finally, SVC visualizes syllabi structures with respect to selected issues.

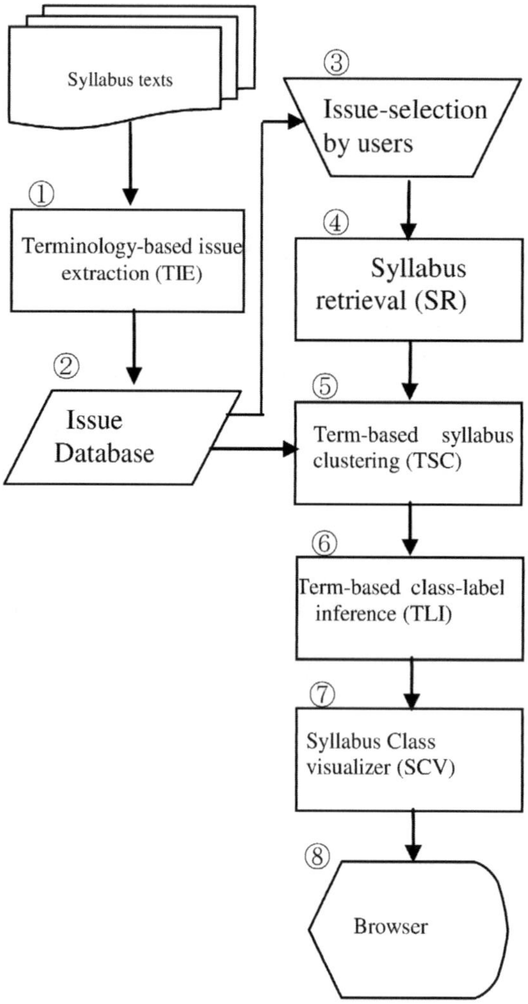

FIGURE 1 – The system diagram

3 Terminological processing as an ontology development

The lack of clear naming standards within a domain (e.g., biomedicine) makes ATR a non-trivial problem (Fukuda et al., 1998). Also, this lack of standards may typically cause many-to-many relationships between terms and concepts. In practice, two problems stem from this issue: (1) some terms may have multiple meanings (i.e., *term ambiguity*), and, conversely, (2) some terms may refer to the same concept (i.e., *term variation*). Generally, term ambiguity exerts negative effects on IE precision; term variation decreases IE recall. These problems reveal the difficulty involved in the use of simple keyword-based IE techniques. Therefore, the development of more sophisticated techniques, such as the identification of groups of different terms that refer to the same (or similar) concept(s) that could benefit from reliance on efficient and consistent ATR/ATC and term variation management methods, is needed. These methods are also important tools that can be used to organize domain-specific knowledge because terms should not be treated

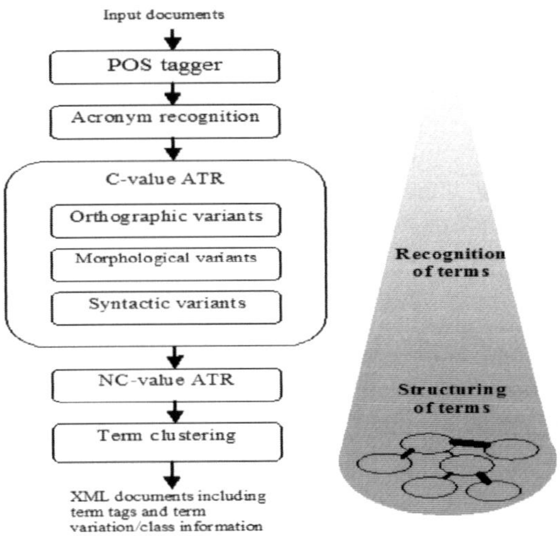

FIGURE 2 – Term recognition as issue extraction

in isolation from other terms. Rather, they should be related to one another so that relationships that exist between corresponding concepts are, at least partially, reflected in the terminology.

3.1 Term recognition

For our system, we used an ATR method based on *C/NC-value* methods (Mima et al., 2001; Mima and Ananiadou, 2001). The *C-value* method recognizes terms by combining linguistic knowledge and statistical analysis. The method extracts multi-word terms,[2] and it is not limited to a specific class of concepts. It is implemented as a two-step procedure. In the first step, term candidates are extracted by the use of a set of linguistic filters that describe general term formation patterns. In the second step, the term candidates are assigned termhood scores (referred to as *C-values*) based on a statistical measure. The measure amalgamates four numerical corpus-based characteristics of a candidate term: (1) frequency of occurrence, (2) frequency of occurrence as a substring of other candidate terms, (3) the number of candidate terms that contain the given candidate term as a substring, and (4) the number of words contained in the candidate term.

The *NC-value method* further improves the *C-value* results by considering the context of the candidate terms. The relevant context words are extracted and assigned weights based on the frequency with which they appear with top-ranked term candidates extracted by the *C-value* method. Subsequently, context factors are assigned to candidate terms according to their co-occurrence with top-ranked context words. Finally, new termhood estimations, referred to as *NC-values*, are calculated as a linear combination of the *C-values* and context factors for the respective terms. Evaluation of the *C/NC-methods* (Mima and Ananiadou, 2001) has revealed that contextual information improves term distribution in the extracted list because it places real terms closer to the top of the list.

[2] More than 85% of domain-specific terms are multi-word terms (Mima and Ananiadou, 2001).

3.2 Term variation management

Term variation and ambiguity have caused and continue to cause problems for ATR, as well as for human experts. Several methods for term variation management have been developed. For example, the BLAST system (Krauthammer et al., 2000) used approximate text string matching techniques and dictionaries to recognize spelling variations in gene and protein names. FASTR (Jacquemin, 2001) handles morphological and syntactic variations by means of meta-rules used to describe term normalization. Semantic variants are handled via WordNet.

The basic *C-value* method has been enhanced by term variation management (Mima and Ananiadou, 2001). We consider a variety of sources from which term variation problems originate. In particular, we deal with orthographical, morphological, syntactic, lexico-semantic, and pragmatic phenomena. Our approach to term variation management is based on term normalization as an integral part of the ATR process. Term variants (i.e., synonymous terms) are addressed in the initial phase of ATR when term candidates are singled out. This differs from the process that is used in other approaches (e.g., FASTR handles variants subsequently by application of transformation rules to extracted terms). Each term variant is normalized (see, Table 1, as an example) and term variants that have the same normalized form are then grouped into classes to link each term candidate to all of its variants. In this way, a list of normalized term candidate classes, rather than a list of single terms, is statistically processed. The termhood is then calculated for a whole class of term variants, rather than for each term variant separately.

Term variants	Normalized term
human cancers cancer in humans human's cancer human carcinoma	→ human cancer

TABLE 1 – Automatic term normalization

3.3 Term clustering

In addition to term recognition, term clustering is an indispensable component of the literature mining process. Because terminological opacity and polysemy are very common in molecular biology and biomedicine, term clustering is essential for the semantic integration of terms, the construction of domain ontologies, and for semantic tagging.

In our system, ATC is performed by the use of a hierarchical clustering method in which clusters are merged based on average mutual information that measures the strength of the relationships between terms (Ushioda, 1996). The system uses terms automatically recognized by the *NC-value* method and their co-occurrences as input. A dendrogram of terms is produced as output. Parallel symmetric processing is used for high-speed clustering. The calculated term cluster information is encoded and used for calculation of semantic similarities in the SCE component. More precisely, the similarity between two individual terms is determined based on their position in a dendrogram. In addition, a commonality measure is defined as the number of shared ancestors between two terms in the dendrogram. A positional measure is defined as the sum of their distances from the root. Similarity between two terms corresponds to a ratio between commonality and positional measure.

Table 3 shows a sample of automatically-recognized terms (issues) that occur in an Engineering domain syllabus text that consists of 850 lectures (Faculty of Engineering, University of Tokyo, 2006). As we can see from the Table, reasonable and representative issues were successfully extracted by our method.

Automatically-Recognized Terms	Termhood
基礎知識 (basic knowledge)	144.55
線形代数 (linear algebra)	77.35
統計力学 (statistical mechanics)	74.00
固体物理 (solid-state physics)	67.20
ベクトル解析 (vector calculus)	65.01
偏微分方程式 (partial differential equation)	62.40
材料力学 (mechanics of materials)	62.13
環境問題 (environmental issues)	60.17

TABLE 2 – Sample of recognized issues

Further details of the methods and their evaluations can be found in Mima et al. (2001) and Mima and Ananiadou (2001).

4 The Use of Visualization to Generate Issue-oriented Syllabus Structures

In our system, the TSC, TLI, and SCV are implemented by the integration of terminology-based issue extraction from syllabi and by clustering of syllabi based on semantic similarities that are also calculated based on terms in syllabi. Graph-based visualization for the automatic generation of issue-oriented syllabus structures is also provided to help in retrieval of lectures. Figure 3 shows an example of the visualization of issue-oriented syllabus structures relevant to the issue, "environment and energy," that occurs in the engineering syllabus. To structure knowledge, the system constructs a graph in which the nodes are used to indicate relevant syllabi for the key issues selected by the user. Links among the syllabi indicate semantic similarities that are calculated by the use of terminological information developed by our TIE components. Semantic similarity is based on comparisons of terminological information extracted from each syllabus, whereas conventional similarity calculation is generally based on extracted nouns. In addition, the locations of each node are calculated and optimized when the graph is drawn. The distance between nodes depends on the closeness of their meanings. The complete algorithm of this issue-structuring method is presented below:

```
begin
  Q ← issues specified to IR
  R ← IR(Q)  // retrieving relevant syllabi to Q and putting them into R
  for every x in R do
    w(Q, x) ← IRscore(Q, x)  // calculate IR score between Q and x
    for every y in R do
      if x ≠ y then
          p ← Ont(x)  // retrieving terminological information of x
          q ← Ont(y)  //          "                    y
          w(x,y) ← Sim(p,q)  // calculate similarity using p and q
      fi
    end
  end
  Visualize graph based on every {w(i,j)|i=Q or i∈R, j∈R, i≠j}
end.
```

We generate an issue-oriented syllabus structure based on (1) cluster recognition and (2) terminology-based cluster label inference. Cluster recognition is performed by detection of groups of nodes in which every combination of included nodes is strongly linked (i.e., their similarity exceeds a threshold). Automatic cluster label inference is performed by the use of terminological information included in each cluster with respect to tf (term frequency) and df (document frequency (i.e., term generality)).

5 Evaluation

We performed a practical application of the system for syllabus retrieval for the University of Tokyo's Online Course Catalogue (UTOCC),[3] for the Open Course Ware (UT-OCW)[4] site, and for the syllabus-structuring (SS) site[5] for the School/Department of Engineering. All of these syllabi are available to the public over the Internet. The UT-OCW's course search system is designed to search the syllabi of courses posted on the UT-OCW site and on the Massachusetts Institute of Technology's OCW site (MIT-OCW). In addition, OCC and SS site's search is designed to search the syllabi of more than 9,000 lectures from all schools/departments at the University of Tokyo, and 1,600 lectures from the School/Department of Engineering at the University of Tokyo. Both systems display search results based on relationships that exist among the syllabi as a structural graphic (see, Figure 3). Based on terms that were automatically-extracted terms (issues) from the syllabi and on similarities calculated by the use of those terms, the system displays the search results in a network format that uses dots and lines. In other words,

[3] http://catalog.he.u-tokyo.ac.jp/
[4] http://ocw.u-tokyo.ac.jp/.
[5] http://ciee.t.u-tokyo.ac.jp/.

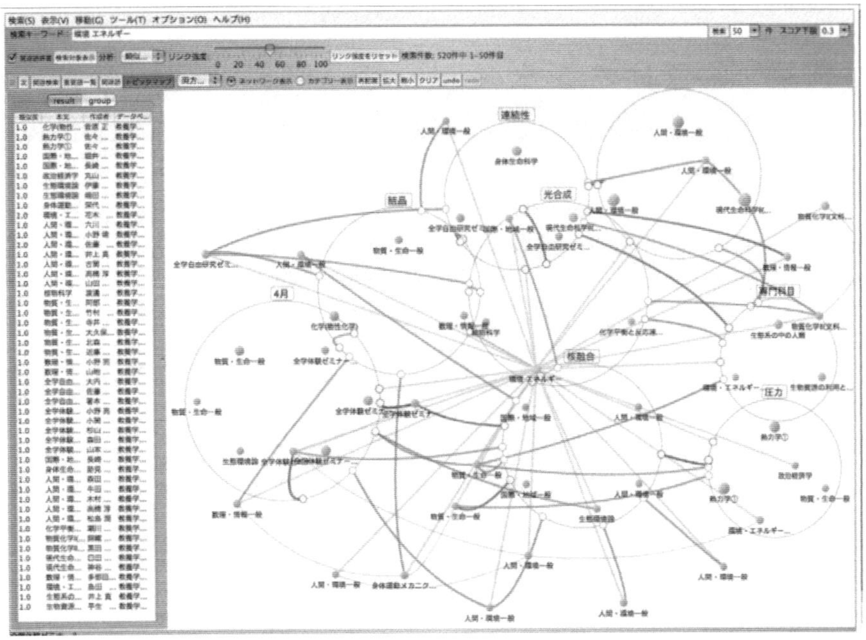

FIGURE 3 – Issue-oriented syllabus structuring: Visualization sample

the system extracts issues from the listed syllabi. It rearranges these syllabi based on semantic relationships that occur in the contents. It displays the results graphically. This differs from conventional search engines that simply list syllabi related to keywords. Because of this process, we believe users will be able to search for key information and obtain results in a minimal amount of time. In graphic displays, as mentioned previously, relevant syllabi are shown in a structural graphic that uses dots and lines with cluster circles. Stronger semantic relationships that occur in the syllabi or clusters will be located in closer proximity on the graphic. This structure will enable users to find groups of courses/lectures that are closely related to some issues. It will also help users take courses/lectures in logical order (e.g., a user can begin with fundamental mathematics and proceed to applied mathematics). Furthermore, if they consult the structural graphic display, users will be able to instinctively find relationships among syllabi drawn from other faculties or universities.

Currently, we have obtained over 2,000 hits per day, on average, from sites worldwide. We have provided more than 50,000 page views during the last three months.

We conducted a usability evaluation based on questionnaires used to survey 120 novice students. We obtained positive statements about the efficiency of syllabus retrieval by the search system from more than 70% of respondents.

Finally, we obtained 151 positive statements and 168 statements that recommended further improvement. Tables 3 and 4 demonstrate the breakdown for positive statements and the breakdown for statements that recommended further improvement, respectively. As can be seen in Table 3, we can reasonably state that our issue-oriented scheme and the related system is relatively efficient at syllabus retrieval. On the other hand, as can be seen in Table 4, we must continue to make further improvements. In particular, we must improve the visualization scheme and its scalability to link other syllabi DB and systems.

Positive statements	#
Advantage of visualization	45
Improvement in retrieval efficiency	41
Clarity of results	22
User-friendly interfaces	20
Misc.	23
Total	151

TABLE 3 – Breakdown of positive statements

Statements that recommended further improvement	#
Complexity of visualization	67
Additional linkage to other syllabi	23
Lack of clarity about relationships that exist among lectures	11
Linkage to other systems (e.g., lecture management, etc.)	13
Quality of issue extraction	10
Difficulty of operation	5
Speed of calculation	1
Misc.	38
Total	168

TABLE 4 – Statements that recommend further improvement

Conclusion

We developed an issue-oriented syllabus retrieval system that combined terminological processing, information retrieval, similarity calculation-based document clustering, and visualization. The system provides visualizations of issue-oriented syllabus structuring during retrieval. This differs from conventional syllabus retrieval that solely provides a list of retrieved results relevant to a specific query.

We evaluated the system based on data collected from questionnaires used to survey over 100 students. Based on our results, we can reasonably state that the system provides relatively efficient syllabus retrieval.

References

Fukuda, K., Tsunoda, T., Tamura, A. and Takagi, T. (1998). *Toward information extraction: Identifying protein names from biological papers*, Proc. of PSB-98, Hawaii, pp. 3:705–716.

Mima, H., Ananiadou, S. and Matsushima, K. (2006). *Terminology-based Knowledge Mining for New Knowledge Discovery, ACM Transactions on Asian Language Information Processing* (TALIP), Vol. 5(1), pp. 74–88.

Mima, H., Ananiadou, S. and Nenadic, G. (2001). *ATRACT workbench: An automatic term recognition and clustering of terms.* In V. Matoušek, P. Mautner, R. Moučkek, K. Taušer (eds.) Text, Speech and Dialogue, LNAI 2166, Springer Verlag, pp. 126–133.

Mima, H. and Ananiadou, S. (2001). *An application and evaluation of the C/NC-value approach for the automatic term recognition of multi-word units in Japanese, International Journal of Terminology*, Vol. 6(2), pp. 175–194.

Krauthammer, M., Rzhetsky, A., Morozov, P. and Friedman, C. (2000). *Using BLAST for identifying gene and protein names in journal articles. Gene* 259, pp. 245–252.

Jacquemin, C. (2001). *Spotting and discovering terms through NLP.* MIT Press, Cambridge MA, p. 378.

Ushioda, A. (1996). *Hierarchical clustering of words.* In Proc. of COLING '96, Copenhagen, Denmark, pp. 1159–1162.

Real-Time Tone Recognition in A Computer-Assisted Language Learning System for German Learners of Mandarin

Hussein HUSSEIN[1] *Hansjörg MIXDORFF*[2] *Rüdiger HOFFMANN*[1]
(1) Chair for System Theory and Speech Technology, Dresden University of Technology, Dresden, Germany
(2) Department of Computer Sciences and Media, Beuth University of Applied Sciences, Berlin, Germany
hussein.hussein@mailbox.tu-dresden.de, mixdorff@beuth-hochschule.de

ABSTRACT
This paper presents an evaluation of tone recognition systems integrated in a computer-assisted pronunciation training system for German learners of Mandarin. Both the reference tone recognition system as well as a recently redesigned tone recognition system contain monotone, bitone and tritone recognizers for isolated monosyllabic and disyllabic words and sentences, respectively. The performance of the reference system and the redesigned tone recognition systems was compared on data from German learners of Mandarin, while varying the feature vector to contain spectral as well as prosodic features. The redesigned tone recognition system matched or outperformed the reference system. For monosyllabic and disyllabic words it improved when spectral features were added to prosodic features. In contrast, results of tone recognition in sentences yielded better results based on prosodic features only.

KEYWORDS: Mandarin Chinese, Tone Recognition, Computer-Assisted Language Learning.

1 Introduction

It is commonly known that Mandarin or standard Chinese is a tone language and hence tonal contours of syllables change the meaning. There are 22 consonant initials (including glottal stop) and 39 vowel finals. Mandarin comprises a relatively small number of syllables. The most important acoustic correlate of tones is F_0. Mandarin has four syllabic tones, that is, high, rising, low, and falling (Tones 1-4) and a neutral tone (Tone 0) in unstressed syllables. In citation forms of monosyllabic words the tonal patterns are very distinct as shown in figure 1, but when several syllables are connected, F_0 contours observed vary considerably due to tonal coarticulation. German is a stress-timed non-tonal language. Mandarin differs from German on the segmental level, but it is the tonal distinctions that pose serious problems to German learners, especially in the context of two or more syllables. Therefore tone display, recognition and correction are paramount features for a pronunciation training system. In the current paper we present results from a redesigned tone recognition system intended to bring improvement over the reference approach employed in the computer-assisted pronunciation teaching (CAPT) system so far.

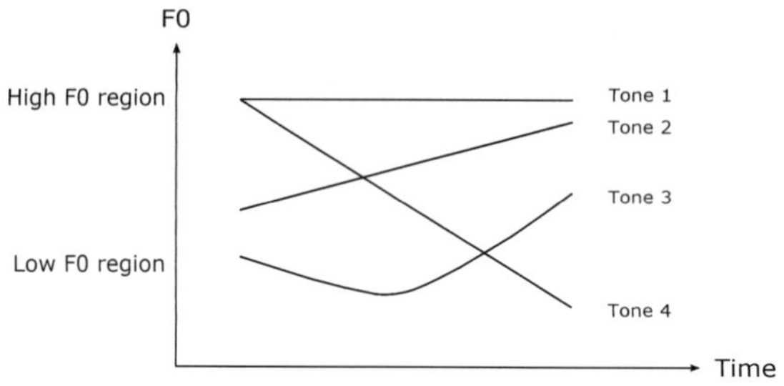

Figure 1: Typical F_0 patterns of Tones 1-4 in mono-syllables.

Robust feature extraction and tone modeling techniques are required for reliable tone recognition algorithms. Accuracy of tone recognition obtained on isolated words is typically high, but deteriorates on continuous speech. This implies that hitherto most speech recognition systems for tone languages only rely on spectral features, because they can be estimated more reliably than prosodic features. Many statistical methods for Mandarin tone recognition have been proposed, including Hidden Markov Models (HMM), Neural Networks (NN), Decision-tree classification, Support Vector Machines (SVM) and rule-based methods (Chen and Jang, 2008)(Liao et al., 2010). Most tone recognition algorithms use F_0 contours as basic features. The accuracy of tone recognition for Tones 1-4 is usually high, but much lower for the neutral tone, because F_0 features are not effective to discriminate the neutral tone. Energy, however, has been found to be an effective cue for tone perception when F_0 is missing.

Taking into account tonal coarticulation in the context of the Computer-Assisted Language Learning (CALL) system for German learners of Mandarin (*"CALL-Mandarin system"*), tone recognition systems consisting of monotone, bitone and tritone recognizers were integrated. Whereas a monotone model operates on isolated syllables, a bitone model takes into consideration the tone of the left neighboring syllable and a tritone model depends on the tones of both the left and right neighboring syllables. The reference tone recognition system of our project partner (IFLYTEK company, Hefei, China) and the redesigned system consist of monotone and bitone recognizers for isolated monosyllabic and disyllabic words as well as a tritone-based continuous speech recognizer for sentences. They were evaluated on data from German leaners of Mandarin.

2 Speech Material

2.1 Chinese Data - L1

The experiments of speaker-independent tone recognition were carried out using three read speech databases from native speakers of Mandarin ("*CN_Mono*", "*CN_Bi*" and "*CN_Sent*").

1. ***CN_Mono* - Isolated Monosyllabic Words:**
   The monotone recognizer was trained on isolated monosyllabic words. The monosyllables were uttered by 29 female and 27 male native speakers of Mandarin, yielding a total of 45000 monosyllables (14.83 hours).
2. ***CN_Bi* - Isolated Disyllabic Words:**
   The bitone recognizer was trained with isolated disyllabic words. The disyllabic words were produced by the same native speakers as in *CN_Mono* with a total of 75000 disyllables (28.83 hours).
3. ***CN_Sent* - Sentences:**
   The tritone recognizer was trained on sentence data. The sentences were produced by 200 native speakers of Mandarin with a total of 2023 utterances (18.60 hours). Each utterance contains a recording of one paragraph composed of several long sentences with a minimum of 11 and a maximum of 231 syllables. The average length of a paragraph is about 115 syllables.

2.2 German Data - L2

Three speech databases from German learners of Mandarin ("*DE_Mono*", "*DE_Bi*" and "*DE_Sent*") were used for the evaluation of tone recognizers by German learners of Mandarin in real-time. The amount of these data is rather small, but they include all available data which are not used in the adaptation process.

1. ***DE_Mono* - Isolated Monosyllabic Words:**
   DE_Mono consists of eight monosyllabic words produced by 5 German learners with a total of 40 utterances.
2. ***DE_Bi* - Isolated Disyllabic Words:**
   DE_Bi consists of 10 disyllabic words produced by 12 German students yielding a total of 120 utterances.
3. ***DE_Sent* - Sentences:**
   DE_Sent consists of 10 sentences produced by 12 German students with a total of 120 utterances.

3 Tone Recognition

In order for tone recognition to take place the utterance must be segmented on the syllable and phone levels. This task is performed by the phone recognizer of iFlyTek for both the reference and redesigned tone recognition system.

3.1 Reference Recognizer

The tone recognition system of iFlyTek is part of an automated proficiency test of Mandarin. (Wang et al., 2007). F_0 contours are calculated with the Praat default algorithm

(Boersma and Weenink, 2001). Tone models consist of four emitting states for monotone, bitone and tritone models. HMMs were employed for tone modeling. The training data, which is different from the data described in section 2.1, consists of utterances from native speakers of Mandarin (164 female and 105 male speakers, 30 minutes for each speaker).

3.2 Redesigned Recognizer

Different kinds of features, including spectral and prosodic-based features, were used. F_0 contours were calculated via the Robust Algorithm for Pitch Tracking (RAPT) (Talkin, 1995). RAPT was modified and integrated in the *CALL-Mandarin system* to work in real-time. The output of RAPT contains in addition to F_0 values, energy (RMS) and voicing (DoV) measures. Since F_0 contours are often affected by extraction errors and micro-prosody, and are interrupted for unvoiced sounds, the raw F_0 data is often pre-processed by applying interpolation and smoothing. In our case we applied a cubic spline interpolation and smoothing and filtered the resulting contour at a stop-frequency of 0.5 Hz yielding a high frequency component (HFC) and a low frequency component (LFC) as in (Mixdorff, 2000). Based on the fact that phrase components should be taken into account when analyzing and synthesizing F_0 contours of Mandarin, it was found that tone recognition results based on HFCs are better than results based on smoothed F_0 contours (Hussein et al., 2012). For the subsequent processing we only used the HFC, thus disregarding low frequency phrase level influences. High frequency contours and energy contours were normalized applying *z-score* normalization. The spectral features, 13 Mel-Frequency Cepstral Coefficients (MFCCs) and their deltas and delta-deltas were also used for tone recognition. All features were only extracted from the final segments. We compared the performance of several feature vectors:

- A: F_0-based features.
- B: F_0- and energy-based features.
- C: F_0-, energy-based and voicing features. These features refer to prosodic features.
- D: MFCC-based features.
- E: MFCC-, F_0-, energy-based and voicing features.

HMMs were employed for tone modeling. The tone models consist of three emitting states for monotone, bitone and tritone models. 64 mixtures were used for cases A, B and C and 512 mixtures for cases D and E. The data *CN_Mono*, *CN_Bi* and *CN_Sent* were used for the training of the monotone, bitone and tritone models, respectively. Every database was divided into training data (90%) and test data (10%). Since there will be insufficient data associated with many of the states, similar acoustic states within bitone or tritone sets were tied to ensure that all state distributions were robustly estimated. The number of Gaussian components in each mixture was increased iteratively during training. Six iterations gave the best results for cases A, B and C. 16 and 20 iterations gave the best results for cases D and E, respectively. Tone models were adapted by using German students' data labeled as correct by Chinese native listeners Maximum Likelihood Linear Regression (MLLR) was implemented for the adaptation of tone models.

3.3 Evaluation of Mandarin Tone Recognition

Two experiments were performed. First, we tested the redesigned recognition system on data *CN_Mono*, *CN_Bi* and *CN_Sent* from native speakers of Mandarin and compared the performance on feature vectors A-E. This test was run outside the CAPT system. Second, we compared the reference system with two versions of the redesigned system after integrating them into the CAPT system, on data *DE_Mono*, *DE_Bi* and *DE_Sent* from German learners of Mandarin:

- R: Tone recognizer by iFlyTek (reference).
- C′: Tone recognizer using prosodic features (case C) and adapted tone models.
- E′: Tone recognizer using both spectral and prosodic features (case E) and adapted tone models.

4 Experimental Results

The correctness of the three tone recognizers trained on feature sets A to E is displayed in table 1. The table shows that adding energy and voicing features to F_0 features (case C) improved the tone recognition results. The combination of spectral and prosodic features (case E) improved the tone correctness in comparison to individual features, especially in tone recognition of sentences. Tone correctness for monotone, bitone and tritone recognizers is 99.50%, 98.86% and 77.03% using both spectral and prosodic features for monosyllables, disyllables and sentences, respectively. The result of the bitone recognizer only concerns the recognition of Tones 1-4, since the data *CN_Bi* did not contain neutral tone.

Feature	*CN_Mono*	*CN_Bi*	*CN_Sent*
A	81.53	94.69	63.79
B	96.28	96.90	66.68
C	97.39	97.31	67.37
D	97.36	93.90	58.68
E	99.50	98.86	77.03

Table 1: Tone correctness of monotone, bitone and tritone recognizers by using different kinds of features and normalized HFCs on data by native speakers of Mandarin (in %).

Figure 2 presents the tone evaluation results of monotone, bitone and tritone recognizers for the reference tone recognizer (R) and the redesigned tone recognizers when applying prosodic features (C′) and combined spectral and prosodic features (E′). The monotone, bitone and tritone recognizers were tested in the *CALL-Mandarin system* by using the data *DE_Mono*, *DE_Bi* and *DE_Sent*, respectively. The tone correctness of monosyllables in R and E′ is the same. The tone recognition in monosyllabic words using both spectral and prosodic features improved the results significantly in comparison to prosodic features only. On disyllabic words, the bitone recognizer based on the combination of spectral and prosodic features outperformed the other presented algorithm. In contrast, for sentence recognition, the tritone recognizer based only on prosodic features outperformed the other algorithms. This result suggests that the variation in the MFCCs which is mostly due to segmental and not tonal variations affects the tritone models more than the monotone and bitone models.

Conclusions

This study compared redesigned monotone, bitone and tritone HMM-based Mandarin tone recognizers for our CALL system for German learners of Mandarin with a pre-exisiting reference. During development different spectral and prosodic features were tested. Of the F_0

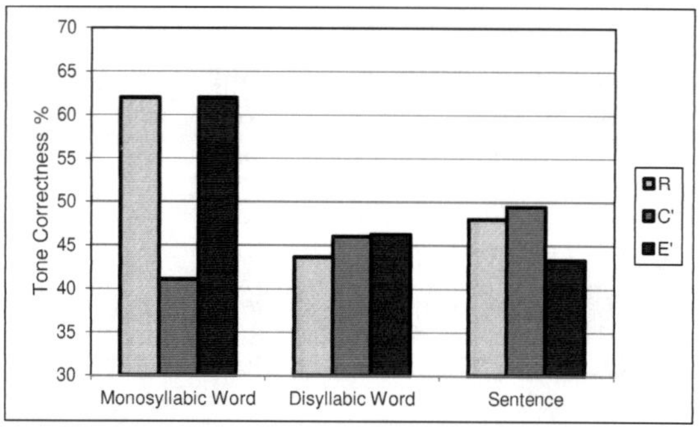

Figure 2: Tone correctness of monotone, bitone and tritone recognizers for reference (R) and redesigned tone recognizers (C′ and E′) on data by German learners of Mandarin in *CALL-Mandarin system*.

contour we only employed the HFC, hence suppressing phrasal contributions. The tone models were adapted by using correct data from German learners of Mandarin. Tone recognition of mono- and disyllabic words using both spectral and prosodic features yielded the best results. In contrast, for sentence recognition the tritone recognizer based on only prosodic features performed best. Overall, the redesigned tone recognition system matched or surpassed the performance of the reference system and will therefore henceforth be employed in the CALL system. Including the new features slightly increases the computation time of the system which, however, as informal tests have shown, is still short enough to provide online feedback.

Acknowledgements

This work is funded by the German Ministry of Education and Research grant 1746X08 and supported by DAAD-NSC and DAAD-CSC project related travel grants for 2009/2010.

References

Boersma, P. and Weenink, D. (2001). Praat: doing phonetics by computer.

Chen, J.-C. and Jang, J.-S. R. (2008). TRUES: Tone Recognition Using Extended Segments. *ACM Transactions on Asian Language Information Processing*, 7(3).

Hussein, H., Mixdorff, H., Liao, Y.-F., and Hoffmann, R. (2012). HMM-Based Mandarin Tone Recognition - Application in Computer-Aided Language Learning System for Mandarin. In *Proc. of ESSV*, pages 347–354, Cottbus, Germany. TUDpress.

Liao, H.-C., Chen, J.-C., Chang, S.-C., Guan, Y.-H., and Lee, C.-H. (2010). Decision Tree Based Tone Modeling with Corrective Feedbacks for Automatic Mandarin Tone Assessment. In *Proc. of Interspeech*, pages 602–605, Makuhari, Chiba, Japan.

Mixdorff, H. (2000). A Novel Approach to the Fully Automatic Extraction of Fujisaki Model Parameters. In *Proc. of ICASSP*, volume 3, pages 1281–1284, Istanbul, Turkey.

Talkin, D. (1995). *Speech Coding and Synthesis*, chapter A Robust Algorithm for Pitch Tracking (RAPT), pages 495–518. Elsevier Science, New York, USA.

Wang, R.-H., Liu, Q., and Wei, S. (2007). *Advances in Chinese Spoken Language Processing*, chapter Putonghua Proficiency Test and Evaluation, pages 407–429.

Textbook Construction from Lecture Transcripts

Aliabbas Petiwala Kannan Moudgalya Pushpak Bhattacharya
IIT Bombay , Mumbai India
aliabbas@iitb.ac.in,kannan@iitb.ac.in,pb@cse.iitb.ac.in

ABSTRACT
This paper presents ongoing work on the proposal for Techniques for Construction of Pedagogically Sound Syllabus Guided Textbooks through Quality Courses and Collaboration using collaborative platforms like Wikis, customized Open Educational Resources (OER) and natural language processing technologies.The course videos from NPTEL at IITs are quality courses presented by leading faculties of IITs. The problem with such rich video courses is the question of usability of the courses, it would be nice if there would exist a textbook companion for these courses customized to the syllabus of the student's home university. This will save the student's time by enabling the student to study only what is required to be studied and thus provide a customized textbook catering to the respective university syllabus or even allowing the student to generate ones own personalized textbook companion for the video courses.A suitable platform needs to be developed which would act as a central repository for collaboratively organizing, indexing and proper interfacing of these Instructional material. A major goal of this platform should be to generate customized textbooks according to the syllabus.

KEYWORDS: Textbooks, lecture transcript, NLP, Authoring.

1 Introduction

In today's world of Open Online Universities, video lectures and OER from eminent professors around the world, high quality lecture video has become easily available to the student. The major problem in creation of OER is how useful it is to the user community. Different universities have substantially different syllabus for the same course. The videos available for each course even have surprisingly different content. Its a common case when students require certain parts of the course which is taught at the user's home university is not available in the course lectures and similarly it is possible that a student who is not interested in some topics and yet he inadvertently goes through the non topics which are not taught at the home university.

Also,What if a student is interested only in parts of the video lectures. If a topic required in his exam is missing in the course, how does he find it? Is there a textbook that goes with the video lecture? To answer these questions and to make the learning material widely useful, we propose a textbook project.

2 Related Work

None of the previous work on textbook generation discussed explores the possibility of customized automatic textbook generation based on syllabus by an authoritative instructor.An important distinction from the work of ebook generation from web (Chen et al., 2005) and connexions project (Henry et al., 2003) is that we require to generate the textbook from the Wiki course content repository which is closely moderated and compiled by the instructor.

3 The Textbook Authoring Platform

The proposed solution to the mentioned problem can be depicted by the data flow diagram in Fig.1.Although a good portion of the textbook is expected to be generated automatically, a substantial amount of manual intervention is also expected, at least at the initial stages to ensure quality. It is likely that some material required for the syllabus of a university may not be present in the wiki. Through the moderation-collaboration route mentioned earlier, the missing information can be added.

A brief Outline of the proposed methodology the TextBook Project are:

1. Convert course lecture transcripts + reference materials of IIT professors to a semantic format like wiki, cnxml, eLML etc
2. Make this available to Subject matter experts over a Wiki. The experts will add\mix \match new information going through a thorough review process.
3. The content for each course is stored in a semantic repository that would grow phenomenally over time.The contents of the course in this repository will be the union of all similar named courses taught at different universities across India.
4. Use a syllabus tool to force the Instructors to submit a detailed syllabus for their course.
5. The syllabus tool would allow instructors to specify detailed meta info about the course like keywords, non topics,beyond scope topics, chapter difficulty,length etc.
6. Extract the information guided by the syllabus to generate a book for that syllabus performing extractive and logical summarization on the fly. The syllabus keywords or used to recommend the most promising text segment from the lecture transcript for the given topic. Many of the existing available techniques(Chandrasekar et al., 1996)(Fujii et al., 2008) (Das & Martins, 2007). can be used to simplify and reorganize the text.The techniques described by (Siddharthan, 2006) can be used for syntactic simplification

and retaining discourse cohesion of the rewritten text. Linguistic problems attacked in the techniques would be simplifying sentences, deciding determiners, deciding sentence order and preserving rhetorical and anaphoric structure.

7. This expanded course will help generate several textbooks corresponding to the syllabi of various Indian universities.
8. The repositories are open to collaboration under strict control of the Wiki Moderator\Teaching Asst. and Instructors.
9. This will help resulting in better transparency , standardization and openness of what is taught across different universities and ease the student in finding the right content according to custom requirements easily.

4 Results and Contributions

This section describes the ongoing work and the contributions made which are on going . The results of applying NLP techniques to the lecture transcripts and textbooks has been discussed in the following sections.

4.1 Applying NLP to Lecture Transcripts Analysis

A corpus of lecture transcripts was constructed containing 40 IIT Bombay lecture transcripts from a basic Electrical Engineering course, 20 MIT lecture transcripts from Introductory AI course and 34 MIT lecture transcripts from physics course. The lecture transcripts were transcribed by a human transcriber. True to our expectation we found that the lecture transcripts seem to incorporate a lot of features which characterize informal active speech which we call it as "lecture speech" .A statistical frequency analysis of the lecture transcripts corpus was done using the NLTK toolkit, and GATE(Cunningham et al., 2011). Following are the prominent features of these lecture transcripts examples are quoted in the parenthesis:

- Frequent use of first and second person ("I", "you")
- Personal references("I will")
- Active voice ("Let's see")
- Simple words and sentences
- Frequent Short sentences
- Interruptions, frequent topic changes and returning back to topics
- Frequent Questioning followed by answer to the posed question by the lecturer himself("What","How")
- Contractions ("wont","lets"...)
- Abbreviations("IIT","Btech")
- Frequent use of demonstrative pronouns to present ideas, slides and examples ('this', 'that', 'there', 'refer', 'see', 'these')

Similarly a textbook corpus was constructed consisting of four famous textbooks in traditional engineering curriculum, each with pages ranging from 300-1500 pages of text. For a textbook we observed that a typical textbook is written in an academically structured and formal style incorporating sound pedagogical principles. A similar statistical frequency analysis on a engineering textbook corpus consisting four authoritative English textbooks in the Engineering domain found the following features:

- Use of Impersonal style (third person:It, that)
- Passive voice(It was found that ...)

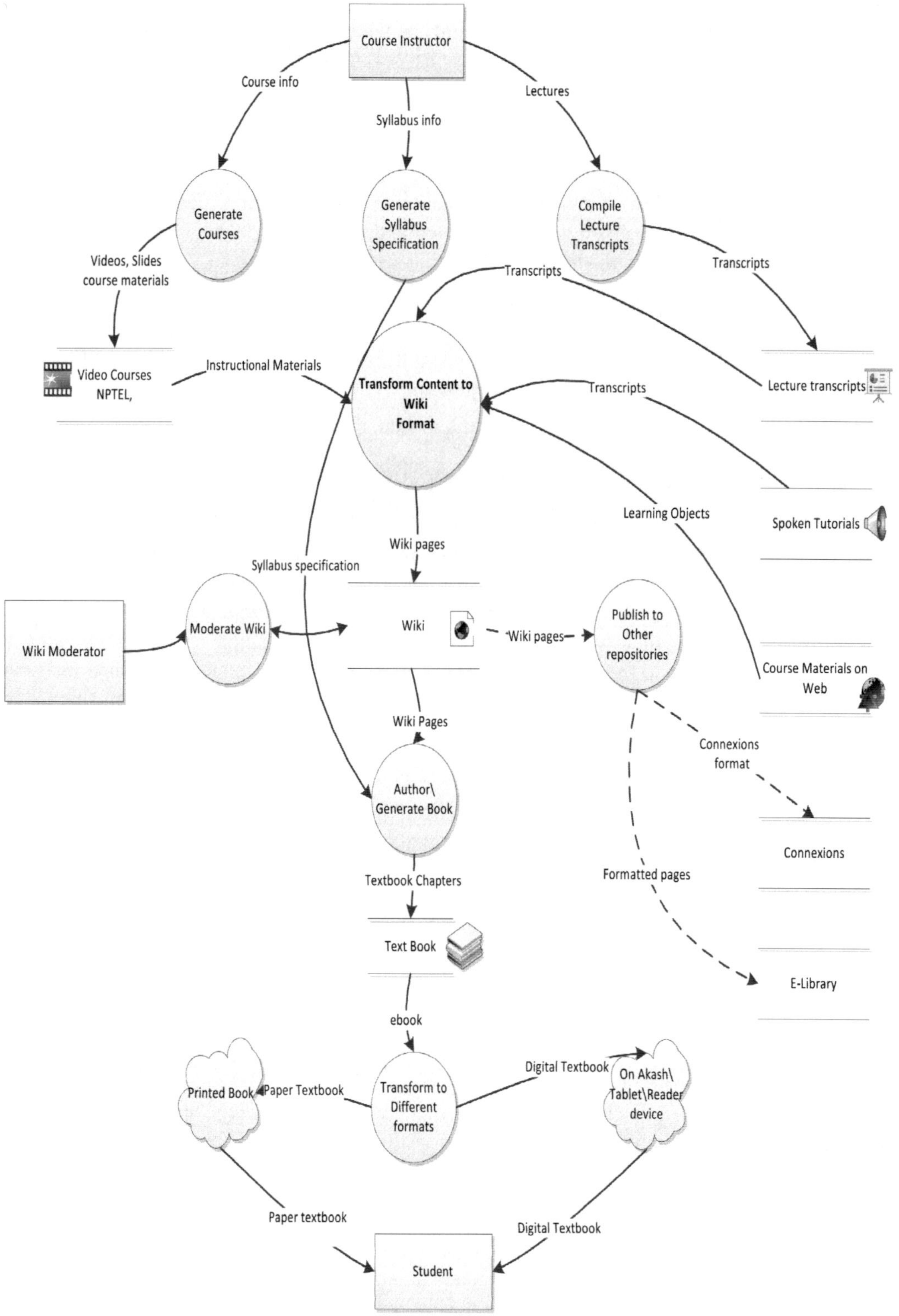

Figure 1: Data flow diagram for TextBook Project

- Reported Speech
- Complex words and sentences to express complex points
- Equations
- Technical jargon
- No contractions
- Use of proper English style , precise education technical vocabulary and several other best practices in literature writing
- Use of objective style, using facts and references to support an argument
- Absence of vague expressions and slang words
- Citations to other books
- Bibliography

The identification of above features of lecture transcripts and textbook content will allow us to define a mapping between the concrete linguistic features of the lecture transcripts and concrete linguistic features of textbooks. It is thus hypothesized that this mapping would help in transforming lecture transcripts to formal textbooks.

A typical lecture transcript contains many unique topics as well as alternating between various topics , need arises to segment the text into relevant cohesive text units and find similarities among them which would help in merging similar sections in the transcript to generate a well structured and coherent text that can serve to achieve the goal of generating a textbook. The following sections elaborate the the techniques and results to find topical changes in the transcripts and its cluster analysis.

4.1.1 Text Segmentation

The text tiling algorithm(Hearst, 1997) was applied to the lecture transcripts and the number of topical segments found in the transcripts is portrayed in Fig 2. The number of segments in the lecture transcripts roughly correspond to the number of topic changes in the lecture. A mean of 14 segments was found per transcript for the EE111 course as shown in the figure.

4.1.2 Clustering to Find and Merge Intra Segment Similarities

The lecture transcripts and for that matter any instructional material contains a lot of redundancy across the entire course. To generate a textbook from the transcripts it is also required to find both inter transcript and intra transcript similarities for the course. The lecture transcripts for each course were clustered to find clusters of similar lecture transcripts that can be probably linked together for better information extraction for textbook generation. A bottom up hierarchical clustering of unsupervised learning was used for cluster analysis. Initially, each transcript is represented as vector of tf-idf features.A tf-idf feature matrix was constructed for all the transcripts assuming each transcript as a document. The bag of words approach was used to compute features of the transcripts. Using a Euclidean distance metrics distances between these vectors of word counts is computed, the closest two texts are grouped into a cluster. The distance from this new cluster to all other transcripts is then recalculated in a recursive fashion. transcripts and clusters are thus compared for similarity, and clustering continues until all transcripts belong to a single top level cluster. The resulting tree can be visualized as a dendrogram. The number of features was empirically fixed at top 50 features ordered by term frequency across the corpus after experimenting with different values for the number of features and fixing a value which optimizes the number of clusters in the hierarchical clustering . The results of this hierarchical clustering was visualized as a dendrogram as shown in Fig.3. The y axis represents the similarity distance between the lecture transcripts at the leaves. It is evident from the dendrogram that the lectures transcripts for each of the lectures are highly successively ordered corresponding to the natural style of the delivered lectures as new vocabulary is introduced as lecture proceeds. These clusters can help us finding similar lectures allowing us to merge similar content. Similarly, to find inter transcript similarities the segments found in the segmentation of the lecture transcripts were clustered to find similar segments across the lecture transcripts for the same course. A tf-idf feature matrix was constructed for all the segments assuming each segment as a document. The number of features was empirically fixed at 50 after experimenting with different values for the number of features and fixing a value which optimizes the number of clusters in the hierarchical clustering . The results of this hierarchical clustering was visualized as a dendrogram as shown in Fig.4. The distinct color bunches of hair in the dendrogram correspond to the clusters of the segments. A zoomed analysis showed that most of the lecture segments are contiguous in natural sequence. This cluster analysis is envisioned for merging, discarding or augmentation of different segments within the transcript for enhancing the coherency and cohesiveness of the target textbook.

Conclusion

We presented the architecture automatic authoring of textbooks from lecture transcripts. This is proposed to be achieved through identifying the features of the transcripts and the textbook and creating a mapping between the two and finally using this mapping to achieve the goal of generating a textbook out of the lecture transcript. Similar segments and cluster analysis results of the transcripts would enable to merge similar topical sections.

References

Chandrasekar, R., Doran, C., & Srinivas, B. (1996). Motivations and methods for text simplification. In *Proceedings of the 16th conference on Computational linguistics-Volume 2* (pp. 1041–1044).

Chen, J., Li, Q., & Jia, W. (2005). Automatically generating an e-textbook on the web. *World Wide Web*, 8, 377–394.

Cunningham, H., Maynard, D., Bontcheva, K., Tablan, V., Aswani, N., Roberts, I., Gorrell, G., Funk, A., Roberts, A., Damljanovic, D., Heitz, T., Greenwood, M. A., Saggion, H., Petrak, J., Li, Y., & Peters, W. (2011). *Text Processing with GATE (Version 6)*.

Das, D. & Martins, A. F. T. (2007). A survey on automatic text summarization. *Literature Survey for the Language and Statistics II course at CMU*, 4, 192–195.

Fujii, Y., Yamamoto, K., Kitaoka, N., & Nakagawa, S. (2008). Class lecture summarization taking into account consecutiveness of important sentences. In *Ninth Annual Conference of the International Speech Communication Association*.

Hearst, M. A. (1997). TextTiling: segmenting text into multi-paragraph subtopic passages. *Computational linguistics*, 23(1), 33–64.

Henry, G., Baraniuk, R., & Kelty, C. (2003). The connexions project: Promoting open sharing of knowledge for education. *Syllabus, Technology for Higher Education*.

Siddharthan, A. (2006). *Syntactic simplification and text cohesion*. PhD thesis.

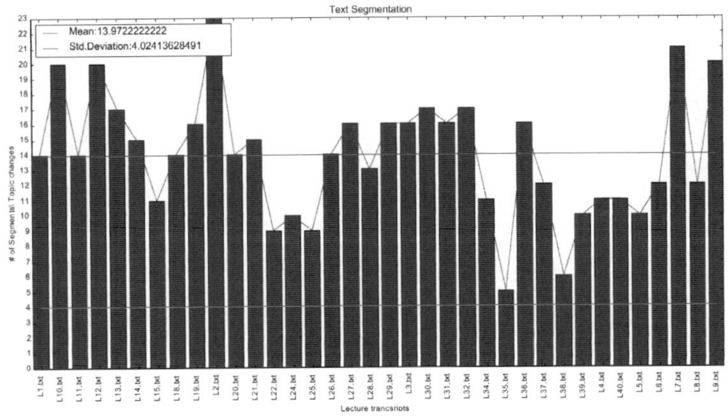

Figure 2: Segmentation Statistics of Lecture Transcripts

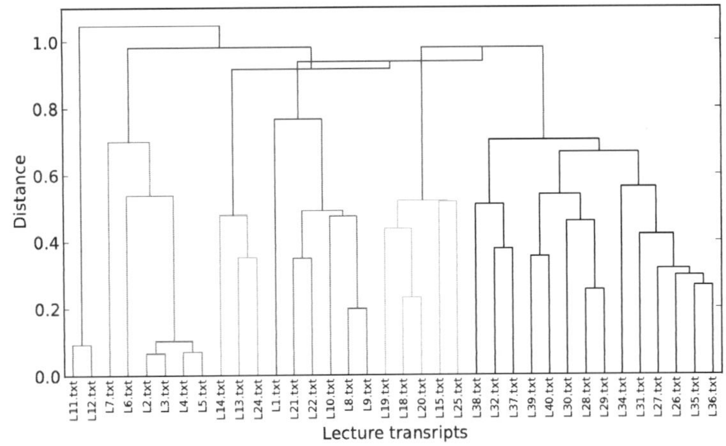

Figure 3: Dendrogram for Hierarchical Clustering of Lecture Transcripts

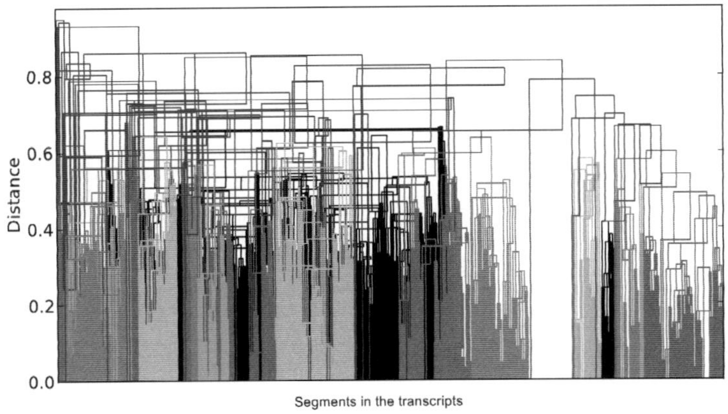

Figure 4: Dendrogram for Text Segment Clustering in the EE lecture Transcripts

Enriching an Academic Knowledge base using Linked Open Data

Chetana Gavankar[1,2] *Ashish Kulkarni*[1]
Yuan-Fang Li[3] *Ganesh Ramakrishnan*[1]
(1) IIT Bombay, Mumbai, India
(2) IITB-Monash Research Academy, Mumbai, India
(3) Monash University, Melbourne, Australia
chetana@cse.iitb.ac.in, kulashish@gmail.com, yuanfang.li@monash.edu, ganesh@cse.iitb.ac.in

ABSTRACT
In this paper we present work done towards populating a domain ontology using a public knowledge base like DBpedia. Using an academic ontology as our target we identify mappings between a subset of its predicates and those in DBpedia and other linked datasets. In the semantic web context, ontology mapping allows linking of independently developed ontologies and inter-operation of heterogeneous resources. Linked open data is an initiative in this direction. We populate our ontology by querying the linked open datasets for extracting instances from these resources. We show how these along with semantic web standards and tools enable us to populate the academic ontology. Resulting instances could then be used as seeds in spirit of the typical bootstrapping paradigm.

KEYWORDS: Ontology Mapping, Academic knowledge base, linked open data, DBpedia.

1 Introduction

Ontologies and knowledge bases play an important role in semantic web. This has led to an independent and distributed effort of developing several domain ontologies and public knowledge bases. In this context, ontology mapping enables interlinking of different ontologies and their population by exploiting similarities between predicates. Prior research discusses several approaches to ontology population ranging from automated to semi-supervised. Bootstrapping approach (Agichtein and Gravano, 2000; Mintz et al., 2009) to ontology population often makes use of a small number of seed examples for each predicate in an ontology. Generating these seeds could benefit from availability of a mapping between a domain ontology and a knowledge base like DBpedia. Using an academic ontology as our target, we study this approach to ontology population and propose a query based formulation to map nodes from the academic ontology to those of the DBpedia ontology. For *e.g.*, *Journal* node from the academic ontology could be mapped to the *Academic Journal* concept in DBpedia. Similarly *Software, Person, Programming Language* etc. have corresponding mappings to nodes in DBpedia.

We will now introduce some basic definitions for setting the context of our work. We will then list the important contributions of our work.

(Flahive et al., 2011) defines *Ontologies* as concepts and relationships used to describe and represent an area of knowledge. An ontology is made up of a set of concepts, properties, property mappings and relationships between the concepts. Concepts are the nodes or objects that identify something that exists. Set of relationships relate two concepts within an ontology. They can either link two concepts together or loop back and link to the same concept. Properties provide extra features used to identify the concept. The property mapping element is similar to a relationship element, but it links a property to a concept rather that one concept to another .

Ontology population primarily concerns itself with the identification of instances for classes in an ontology. It is a knowledge acquisition activity that relies on semi-automatic methods to transform unstructured, semi-structured and structured data sources into instance data.

(Zhang et al., 2012) define *Ontology mapping* as follows. Given two ontologies O_1 and O_2, mapping one ontology onto another means that for each entity *e1* (concept, relation, or instance) in an ontology O_1, we find a corresponding entity *e2*, which has the same intended meaning, in an ontology O_2. $map(e1_i) = e2_j$

The primary contributions of this paper are the following:

- Development of an academic domain ontology.
- Identification of nodes in an academic ontology to be populated using external data sources and mapping to DBpedia ontology nodes.
- Ontology population using SPARQL queries against the DBpedia and other linked datasets.

2 Related Work

We relate our work to the existing work in the area of ontology population to generate academic knowledge base.

Ontology population involves building and populating an ontology from structured, semistructured and unstructured text. There is a large body of work in ontology population (Brunzel,

2008; Poesio and Almuhareb, 2008; Maynard et al., 2008; De Boer et al., 2007) that uses frequency based term extraction along with shallow NLP techniques. However, enterprise data usually does not have the luxury of highly redundant data exploited in the above approaches. Ontology building and population from collaborative resources such as Wikipedia has developed a great interest in researchers across the world. There are various publicly available data sources built using these collaborative resources on the linked data cloud such as YAGO, DBpedia. YAGO2 (Hoffart et al., 2011, 2010; Suchanek et al., 2008; de Melo et al., 2008) is a Geo-spatial ontology built automatically from Wikipedia, GeoNames, and WordNet. It contains 80 million facts about 9.8 million entities. DBpedia data set (Bizer et al., 2009b; Auer et al., 2008; Morsey et al., 2012) consists of RDF triples extracted from the "infoboxes" commonly seen on the right hand side of Wikipedia articles, while Geonames [1] provides RDF descriptions of millions of geographical locations worldwide. These collaborative resources are also used for bootstrapping the ontology population process. Ontological smoothing (Zhang et al., 2012) uses a semi-supervised technique that learns extractors for a set of minimally-labeled relations. It uses the few examples to generate a mapping from the target relation to a database view over a background knowledge base, such as Freebase. It then queries the background knowledge base to retrieve many more instances that are deemed similar to those of the target relation and the system learns the extractor. Our work is influenced the most from this approach. However we choose to use DBpedia and the datasets linked to it as the source knowledge base due to its higher degree of overlap with the academic ontology. We also differ in the mapping technique and write several manual SPARQL queries against the DBpedia SPARQL endpoint[2] to extract instances to be used as seeds in populating the academic ontology.

3 Academic Ontology

Ontology building for a specific domain can start from scratch or by modifying an existing ontology. We built our academic ontology using existing *Benchmark* [3] and *Aisso*[4] ontologies. Ontologies are merged using the *Protege*[5] ontology editor and extended to include several classes like *award, project* etc. and attributes like *professor* has *research-area*, *course* has *prerequisite* etc. In addition, we scraped the glossary lists available in Wikipedia to populate class hierarchy rooted at the *concept* class. An ontology that we finally used consists of more than 190 classes, 150 object properties and 150 data properties. Please refer figure 1 for the snapshot of some nodes in an academic ontology.

4 Ontology Mapping

The preliminary step in extracting instances from external data sources is mapping of nodes in academic ontology with external ontologies. We use ontology mapping between academic ontology and DBpedia ontology. The DBpedia Ontology is hand-made with 205 ontology classes. We first identify the nodes in academic ontology such as *academic conferences* to be populated using an external knowledge bases. We then identify mappings between these nodes and its relational properties with those in DBpedia. The mapping between external data sources and academic ontology involves mapping between nodes, its data properties and object properties. Though the names of concepts in an ontology match, it may not be exact mapping due to

[1] http://www.geonames.org/ontology/
[2] http://dbpedia.org/sparql
[3] http://swat.cse.lehigh.edu/onto/univ-bench.owl
[4] http://vocab.org/aiiso/schema
[5] http://protege.stanford.edu

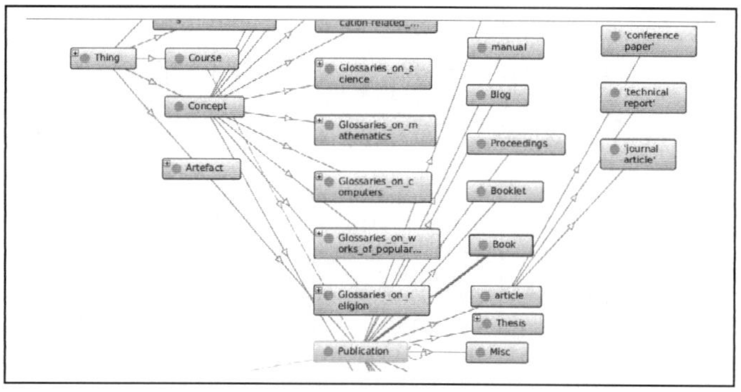

Figure 1: Academic Ontology snapshot of some nodes in ontology

different interpretation in the respective ontologies. Mapping can either be between nodes using equivalence class or subclass or super class relation. All the data properties in the academic ontology may not have corresponding mapping in DBpedia ontology. Conversely all data properties of DBpedia may not have corresponding mapping in Academic ontology like software programming language. There are other issues like the names of label for nodes or property may be different but they mean the same. Example: Label 'location' in DBpedia ontology is same as label 'venue' in academic ontology. Mapping between object property of academic ontology and DBpedia has an additional constraint of checking the domain and range of an object property in both ontologies. We used the above heuristics for ontology mapping between academic ontology and DBpedia ontology. Please refer table 1 for the mapping between academic domain and DBpedia ontology classes.

Academic ontology nodes	DBpedia ontology nodes	Academic ontology properties	DBpedia ontology properties
Book	Book	author, title,abstract, type, date,isbn, publisher	author, title, abstract, type, date, issn, publisher
Event	Event	date, title, location	date, title, venue, event period, committe
Conference	Conference	date, title, location	date, title, venue, event period, committe
Workshop	Workshop	date, title, location	date, title, venue, event period, committe
Journal	AcademicJournal	date, title	publication date, title, ranking
Software	Software	Programming Language, computing platform	Programming Language, computing platform
Programming Language	Programming Language	name	name
Glossaries_on_mathematics	Mathematical_terminology	terms	terms
Glossary_of_graph_theory	Glossary_of_graph_theory	terms	terms
Glossary_of_education-related_terms	Glossary_of_education-related_terms	terms	terms

Table 1: Ontology mapping for sample nodes from Academic ontology to DBpedia ontology

5 Ontology Population

We then search the required entities on linked open data to locate the relevant data source. Due to the openness of this LOD data sources, it is difficult to know data sources relevant for query answering. We use web interface, *open link software* [6] to ease the task of finding relevant data source. The results for a sample search for *glossary of mathematics* are displayed in the figure refer figure 2.

Subsequent to data source searching , we query these resources to extract the relevant instances. Data on the linked open data cloud (Bizer et al., 2009a) are expressed using resource description framework (RDF) or web ontology language OWL. RDF is a directed, labeled graph data format for representing information in the Web. SPARQL protocol and RDF query language (SPARQL)

[6]http://dbpedia.org/fct/

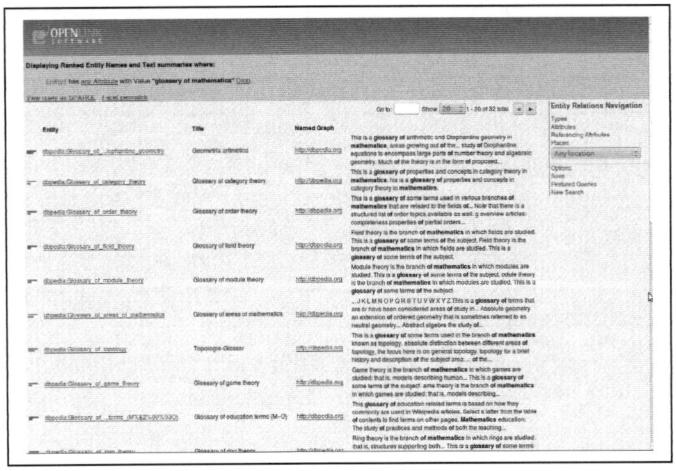

Figure 2: Link open data search results for glossary of mathematics

can be used to express queries across diverse data sources, whether the data is stored natively as RDF or viewed as RDF via middleware. We populate our ontology by querying the linked open datasets using SPARQL for extracting the instances from these RDF resources on the LOD cloud. We wrote and executed SPARQL queries through DBpedia SPARQL endpoint [7]. Refer figure 3 for the results from a sample SPARQL query. The SPARQL queries return a set of instances to populate nodes in academic ontology. Refer Appendix A for set of sample SPARQL queries for extracting instances from linked open data. Resulting instances could then be used as seeds in spirit of the typical bootstrapping paradigm.

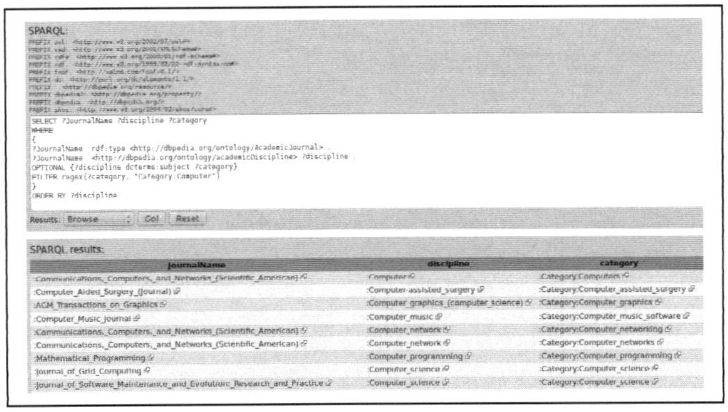

Figure 3: Sample SPARQL query execution

6 Evaluation

The purpose of evaluation was to ascertain the correctness of instances extracted from the linked open data for ontology population. We indexed corpus of three major universities obtained by crawling their pages.We then queried this index for each instance obtained from the linked open data and recorded the top 10 results. We scanned these results to check support for that instance in context of the category being populated. Table 2 summarizes the results of our evaluation for a subset of nodes in our academic ontology [8].

[7]http://dbpedia.org/snorql/

[8]rough estimate for *Softwares* based only on number of search results

Academic ontology node	Extracted	In Corpus	In-context	Precision
AIConferences	7	7	6	0.86
BotanyBooks	32	4	3	0.75
ChemistryJournals	152	94	92	0.98
EngineeringJournals	61	48	42	0.88
ProgramingLanguages	288	183	142	0.78
ComputerScienceConferences	34	26	26	1
ComputerScienceBooks	68	33	18	0.55
GlossaryofMathematics	111	73	58	0.80
GlossaryofMathematicalConcepts	22	18	17	0.95
GlossaryofPredicateLogic	28	11	11	1
Softwares	27947	4386	4326	1

Table 2: Number of instances found in corpus out of the total number of instances obtained by querying linked open data for a subset of nodes in the academic ontology

Conclusion and Future work

In this work, we showed the feasibility of exploiting overlaps between a domain ontology and public knowledge bases using a query based mapping formulation. In particular, we wrote several SPARQL queries against the DBpedia datasets to extract instances for the predicates in our academic ontology. In the process, we studied different types of mappings between ontology predicates ranging from mapping one concept to a combination of many others to mapping different types of predicates. The instances thus extracted could serve as seeds in bootstrapping the ontology population process. That forms the direction of our future research. Such a populated academic knowledge base could be leveraged in information extraction and retrieval applications built over academic corpora.

References

Agichtein, E. and Gravano, L. (2000). Snowball: extracting relations from large plain-text collections. In *Proceedings of the fifth ACM conference on Digital libraries*, DL '00, pages 85–94, New York, NY, USA. ACM.

Auer, S., Bizer, C., Kobilarov, G., Lehmann, J., Cyganiak, R., and Ives, Z. (2008). DBpedia: A nucleus for a web of open data. In *Proceedings of the 6th International Semantic Web Conference (ISWC)*, volume 4825 of *Lecture Notes in Computer Science*, pages 722–735. Springer.

Bizer, C., Heath, T., and Berners-Lee, T. (2009a). Linked data - the story so far. *Int. J. Semantic Web Inf. Syst.*, 5(3):1–22.

Bizer, C., Lehmann, J., Kobilarov, G., Auer, S., Becker, C., Cyganiak, R., and Hellmann, S. (2009b). Dbpedia - a crystallization point for the web of data. *Web Semant.*, 7(3):154–165.

Brunzel, M. (2008). The xtreem methods for ontology learning from web documents. In *Proceedings of the 2008 conference on Ontology Learning and Population: Bridging the Gap between Text and Knowledge*, pages 3–26, Amsterdam, The Netherlands, The Netherlands. IOS Press.

De Boer, V., Van Someren, M., and Wielinga, B. J. (2007). Relation instantiation for ontology population using the web. In *Proceedings of the 29th annual German conference on Artificial intelligence*, KI'06, pages 202–213, Berlin, Heidelberg. Springer-Verlag.

de Melo, G., Suchanek, F. M., and Pease, A. (2008). Integrating YAGO into the Suggested Upper Merged Ontology. In *20th IEEE International Conference on Tools with Artificial Intelligence (ICTAI 2008)*.

Flahive, A., Taniar, D., Rahayu, J. W., and Apduhan, B. O. (2011). Ontology expansion: appending with extracted sub-ontology. *Logic Journal of the IGPL*, 19(5):618–647.

Hoffart, J., Suchanek, F. M., Berberich, K., Lewis-Kelham, E., de Melo, G., and Weikum, G. (2011). Yago2: exploring and querying world knowledge in time, space, context, and many languages. In *Proceedings of the 20th international conference companion on World wide web*, WWW '11, pages 229–232, New York, NY, USA. ACM.

Hoffart, J., Suchanek, F. M., Berberich, K., and Weikum, G. (2010). YAGO2: a spatially and temporally enhanced knowledge base from Wikipedia. Research Report MPI-I-2010-5-007, Max-Planck-Institut für Informatik, Stuhlsatzenhausweg 85, 66123 Saarbrücken, Germany.

Maynard, D., Li, Y., and Peters, W. (2008). Nlp techniques for term extraction and ontology population. In *Proceedings of the 2008 conference on Ontology Learning and Population: Bridging the Gap between Text and Knowledge*, pages 107–127, Amsterdam, The Netherlands, The Netherlands. IOS Press.

Mintz, M., Bills, S., Snow, R., and Jurafsky, D. (2009). Distant supervision for relation extraction without labeled data. In *Proceedings of the Joint Conference of the 47th Annual Meeting of the ACL and the 4th International Joint Conference on Natural Language Processing of the AFNLP: Volume 2 - Volume 2*, ACL '09, pages 1003–1011, Stroudsburg, PA, USA. Association for Computational Linguistics.

Morsey, M., Lehmann, J., Auer, S., Stadler, C., and Hellmann, S. (2012). Dbpedia and the live extraction of structured data from wikipedia. *Program: electronic library and information systems*, 46.

Poesio, M. and Almuhareb, A. (2008). Extracting concept descriptions from the web: the importance of attributes and values. In *Proceedings of the 2008 conference on Ontology Learning and Population: Bridging the Gap between Text and Knowledge*, pages 29–44, Amsterdam, The Netherlands, The Netherlands. IOS Press.

Suchanek, F. M., Kasneci, G., and Weikum, G. (2008). YAGO: A Large Ontology from Wikipedia and WordNet. *Elsevier Journal of Web Semantics*.

Zhang, C., Hoffmann, R., and Weld, D. S. (2012). Ontological smoothing for relation extraction with minimal supervision. In *AAAI*.

A Categories of SPARQL queries

List of computer science conferences. Similar query can be written for other area conferences

```
SELECT ?Conferences
WHERE
```

```
{
?Conferences rdf:type <http://dbpedia.org/class/yago/ComputerScienceConferences> .
}
```

Query for getting list of softwares and details

```
SELECT ?Software ?programmingLanguage ?latestVersion
WHERE
{
?Software rdf:type <http://dbpedia.org/ontology/Software> .
?Software <http://dbpedia.org/ontology/programmingLanguage> ?programmingLanguage .
OPTIONAL {?Software <http://dbpedia.org/property/latestReleaseVersion> ?latestVersion}
}
LIMIT 40
```

Discipline and categories of journal filter using computer. Similarly can be obtained for other categories like physics

```
SELECT ?s ?discipline ?category
WHERE
{
?s rdf:type <http://dbpedia.org/ontology/AcademicJournal> .
?s <http://dbpedia.org/ontology/academicDiscipline> ?discipline .
OPTIONAL ?discipline dcterms:subject ?category
FILTER regex(?category, "Category:Computer")
}
ORDER BY ?discipline
```

Query for list of programming languages

```
SELECT ?ProgrammingLanguage ?version ?OperatingSystem
WHERE
{
?ProgrammingLanguage rdf:type <http://dbpedia.org/ontology/ProgrammingLanguage> .
?ProgrammingLanguage <http://dbpedia.org/ontology/latestReleaseVersion> ?version .
?ProgrammingLanguage <http://dbpedia.org/property/operatingSystem> ?OperatingSystem .
}
LIMIT 100
```

Query for topics along with category and its related category

```
SELECT ?topic ?category ?relatedCategory
WHERE
{
?wikipage foaf:primaryTopic ?topic .
?topic dcterms:subject ?category .
OPTIONAL?category skos:related ?relatedCategory
```

```
FILTER regex(?category, "Category:Computer")
} LIMIT 20
```

To find available category and their broader category

```
SELECT ?isValueOf ?broaderCategory
WHERE
{
?isValueOf rdf:type <http://www.w3.org/2004/02/skos/core#Concept> .
?isValueOf skos:broader ?broaderCategory
}
LIMIT 20
```

Query of list of Academicjournals along with discipline and impact factor

```
SELECT ?s ?d ?i
WHERE
{
?s rdf:type <http://dbpedia.org/ontology/AcademicJournal> .
?s <http://dbpedia.org/ontology/academicDiscipline> ?d
?s <http://dbpedia.org/ontology/impactFactor> ?i
}
ORDER BY ?d
LIMIT 20
```

Query for list of projects

```
SELECT ?projectName ?objective ?keyword ?start ?end ?fundedBy
WHERE
{
?projectName rdf:type <http://dbpedia.org/ontology/Project> .
OPTIONAL{?projectName dbpedia-owl:projectObjective ?objective .}
OPTIONAL{?projectName dbpedia-owl:projectKeyword ?keyword .}
OPTIONAL?projectName dbpedia-owl:projectStartDate ?start .}
OPTIONAL{?projectName dbpedia-owl:projectEndDate ?end.}
OPTIONAL{?projectName dbpedia-owl:fundedBy ?fundedBy .}
}
```

To find all the available disciplines

```
SELECT DISTINCT ?discipline
WHERE
{
?s <http://dbpedia.org/ontology/academicDiscipline> ?discipline .
}
LIMIT 100
```

Finding wikipedia outlinks and redirects

```
SELECT ?resource ?redirects ?outLinks
WHERE { ?resource <http://dbpedia.org/ontology/wikiPageRedirects> ?redirects.
?resource <http://dbpedia.org/ontology/wikiPageExternalLink> ?outLinks
}
LIMIT 20
```

Automatic Pronunciation Evaluation And Mispronunciation Detection Using CMUSphinx

Ronanki Srikanth[1] *Li Bo*[2] *James Salsman*[3]
(1) International Institute of Information Technology, Hyderabad, India
(2) National University of Singapore, Singapore
(3) Talknicer, USA
srikanth.ronanki@research.iiit.ac.in, li-bo@outlook.com, jsalsman@talknicer.com

ABSTRACT
Feedback on pronunciation is vital for spoken language teaching. Automatic pronunciation evaluation and feedback can help non-native speakers to identify their errors, learn sounds and vocabulary, and improve their pronunciation performance. These evaluations commonly rely on automatic speech recognition, which could be performed using Sphinx trained on a database of native exemplar pronunciation and non-native examples of frequent mistakes. Adaptation techniques using target users' enrollment data would yield much better recognition of non-native speech. Pronunciation scores can be calculated for each phoneme, word, and phrase by means of Hidden Markov Model alignment with the phonemes of the expected text. In addition to the basic acoustic alignment scores, we have also adopted the edit distance based criterion to compare the scores of the spoken phrase with those of models for various mispronunciations and alternative correct pronunciations. These scores may be augmented with factors such as expected duration and relative pitch to achieve more accurate agreement with expert phoneticians' average manual subjective pronunciation scores. Such a system is built and documented using the CMU Sphinx3 system and an Adobe Flash microphone recording, HTML/JavaScript, and rtmplite/Python user interface.

KEYWORDS: Pronunciation Evaluation, Text-independent, forced-alignment, edit-distance neighbor phones decoding, CMUSphinx.

1 Introduction

Pronunciation learning is one of the most important parts of second language acquisition. The aim of this work is to utilize automatic speech recognition technology to facilitate learning spoken language and reading skills. Computer Aided Language Learning (CALL) has received a considerable attention in recent years. Many research efforts have been done for improvement of such systems especially in the field of second language teaching. Two desirable features of speech enabled computer-based language learning applications are the ability to recognize accented or mispronounced speech produced by language learners, and the ability to provide meaningful feedback on pronunciation quality.

The paper is organized into the following sections : Section 2 discusses in detail some of the popular and best performing approaches proposed for pronunciation scoring and computer-aided language learning. We present in Section 3 our database preparation for evaluation of the proposed method along with description of TIMIT database used as reference statistics in Text-independent approach and is explained in section 5. Section 4 presents an algorithm to detect mispronunciations based on neighbor phones decoding. Section 5 presents scoring routines for both Text-dependent and Text-independent approaches and finally results are tabulated in section 6 followed by conclusions.

2 Related Work

The EduSpeak system (Franco H. Abrash and J, 2000) is a software development toolkit that enables developers to use speech recognition and pronunciation scoring technology. The paper presents some adaptation techniques to recognize both native and non-native speech in a speaker-independent manner. (L. Neumeyer and Price, 1996) developed automatic Text-independent pronunciation scoring of foreign language student speech by using expert judge scores.

(Seymore and R, 1996) created a system called Fluency (Eskenazi, 2009) to detect and correct foreign speakers pronunciation errors in English. She also used automatic speech recognition to detect pronunciation errors and to provide appropriate correct information.

(Peabody, 2011) focused on the problem of identifying mispronunciations made by non-native speakers using a CALL system. He also proposed a novel method for transforming mel-frequency cepstral coefficients (MFCCs) into a feature space that represents four key positions of English vowel production for robust pronunciation evaluation. (Moustroufas and Digalakis, 2007) presented various techniques to evaluate the pronunciation of students of a foreign language, again without using any knowledge of the uttered text. The authors used native speech corpora for training pronunciation evaluation.

(Sherif Mahdy Abdou and Nazih, 2006) described the implementation of a speech enabled computer-aided pronunciation learning system called HAFSS. The system was developed for teaching Arabic pronunciation to non-native speakers. It used a speech recognizer and a phoneme duration classification algorithm implemented to detect pronunciation errors. The authors also used maximum likelihood linear regression (MLLR) speaker adaptation algorithms.

(Chitralekha Bhat, 2010) designed a pronunciation scoring system using a phone recognizer using both the popular HTK and CMU Sphinx speech recognition toolkits. The system was evaluated on Indian English speech with models trained on the Timit Database. They used forced alignment decoding with both HTK and Sphinx3.

(S. Pakhomov and G.Sales, 2008) and (Eskenazi, 2002) described the measurement of different automatic speech recognition (ASR) technologies applied to the assessment of young children's basic English vocabulary. Former authors used the HTK version 3.4 toolkit for ASR. They calculated acoustic confidence scores using forced alignment and compared those to edit distance between the expected and actual ASR output. They trained three types of phoneme level language models: fixed phonemes, free phonemes and a biphone model.

3 The Data

3.1 Training: TIMIT Data

We used standard TIMIT corpus for training the Text-Independent pronunciation evaluation system and is explained in section 5.2. TIMIT contains broadband recordings of 630 speakers of eight major dialects of American English, each reading ten phonetically rich sentences. The TIMIT corpus includes time-aligned orthographic, phonetic and word transcriptions as well as a 16-bit, 16kHz speech waveform file for each utterance.

3.2 Testing: Data Preparation

We prepared a Non-native database in Indian accent to test the proposed pronunciation evaluation system. The corpus contains recordings of 8 non-native speakers of English from four different regions of India, each reading five sentences and five words. We asked the speakers to pronounce each word 10 times in one complete recording and then mispronounce 10 times either by spelling one of the phones incorrect or by skipping some of the phones in each word, each time. We also asked the speakers to pronounce each sentence 3 times in one complete recording and then mispronounce 3 times by spelling one or more than one word incorrectly. Later, we manually chopped the wav files into recordings of each word, sentence in separate individual files. Thus, we have 400 correct and incorrect recordings of 5 words and 120 correct and incorrect recordings of 5 sentences from 8 Non-Native speakers of English.

4 Edit-distance Neighbor phones decoding

We started our work as to identify the mispronunciations using the help of speech recognition tool Sphinx3. The decoding results shown that both word level and phrase level decoding using Java State Grammar Format (JSGF) are almost same. This method helps to detect the mispronunciations at phone level and to detect homographs as well if the percentage of error in decoding can be reduced.

4.1 Phoneset, Models and Sphinx Decoder

The decoder we used in this paper is Sphinx3_decode which requires either Language Model(LM) or Finite State Grammar(FSG) along with acoustic models trained on large vocabulary database. We used WSJ1 (Lee, 1989) acoustic models for wideband (16kHz) microphone speech, consisting 4000 senone and 32 Gaussian mixtures per stature as Hidden Markov Models (HMM) models to train the system.

Finite State Grammar(FSG) which can be derived from JSGF contains the transition probabilities from one state to another and is supplied as input to the decoder instead of Language model along with acoustic models.

Since we are using CMUSphinx decoder, the phoneset being used in this algorithm is CMU-Arctic phoneset which is also known as CMUbet. Worldbet, CGIbet,ARPAbet are few such other ASCII based phonetic alphabets. Neighboring phones are the list of phones which contains most similar other phonemes for each phoneme in CMUbet. We have chosen the neighbor phones for each phoneme in such a way that the mispronunciation can occur with similar sounding phonemes. For example, the neighbors for phoneme /N/ are (/N/|/M/|/NG/), and /TH/ are (/TH/|/S/|/DH/|/F/|/HH/) etc.,

Along with these. we used CMU dictionary which contains all words in English vocabulary with corresponding representation of phones in CMUbet. In languages like English it is very common to find that the same word can be pronounced in several different ways also known as homographs. The dictionary file in Sphinx is allowed to have several entries for the same word. However, for the system to work properly, the transcription file must state which pronunciation alternative is used for each word. Sphinx provides a way to do this automatically, which is called forced alignment.

4.2 Sphinx Forced-Alignment

The process of force-alignment takes an existing transcript, and finds out which, among the many pronunciations for the words occuring in the transcript, are the correct pronunciations. The output is written into a file with an option phsegdir in sphinx3_align and it contains each phone start and end positions in terms of frames on time scale along with large negative acoustic spectral match score.

SFrm	EFrm	SegAScr	Phone
0	9	-64725	SIL
10	21	-63864	W SIL IH b
22	30	-126819	IH W TH i
31	41	-21470	TH IH SIL e

Table 1: Format of phseg file for a sample word: "WITH"

4.3 Algorithm to detect Mispronunciations

Based on the forced-alignment output, we designed few decoders such as single-phone decoder, word decoder and phrase decoder. Initially, the wav file is chopped into individual phones in case of single-phone decoder, words in case of word decoder and complete phrase is taken in case of phrase decoder. JSGF file is specified in such a way that, each time, the phone is supplied along with its neighbor phones. In single-phone decoder, each phoneme chopped in a separate wav file is decoded along with its neighbor phones. In phrase decoder, all phones along with its neighbor phones is given as input to JSGF. In case of word-decoder, to identify mispronunciation at phone-level, each time only one phoneme is supplied with its neighbor phones keeping the rest constant. For example, word - "WITH" is presented as
public <phonelist> = ((W | L | Y) (IH) (TH));
public <phonelist> = ((W) (IH | IY | AX | EH) (TH));
public <phonelist> = ((W) (IH) (TH | S | DH | F | HH));

The accuracy of each decoder for SA1, SA2 in TIMIT and for some recorded external phrase is reported in Table 2. Both Word decoder and Phrase decoder perform at equal level since the decoding of context-independent phones doesn't vary much across word boundaries. Since, the error-rate can't be negligible even if it is too low, we moved to threshold based scoring method which is explained in next section.

Type	Single-Phone	Word	Phrase
SA1	41.3%	86.1%	84.4%
SA2	42.5%	87%	85.2%
ext. phrase	29%	73.2%	72.1%

Table 2: Decoding Accuracy of each decoder

5 Scoring Routines

5.1 Text-dependent

In Text-dependent approach, we can do pronunciation scoring only for those words/phrases for which we have at least 10-50 native exemplar recordings. This method is completely based on exemplar recordings for each phrase. Initially, Sphinx forced alignment is applied on native exemplar recordings of each phrase in the training dataset. Later, mean acoustic score, mean duration along with standard deviations are calculated for each of the phones in the phrase from the forced-alignment output. Since the acoustic scores are in large negative values, logarithm is applied i.e., log(1-acs) is considered into account where acs is the acoustic score of each phone. Now, given the test recording, each phoneme in the phrase is then compared with exemplar statistics with respect to position of the phoneme in the phrase. The standard score of a raw score x is:

$$z = \frac{x - \mu_i}{\sigma_i} \tag{1}$$

z-scores are calculated from equation (1) for both acoustic score and duration and then normalized scores from 1-5 are calculated based on maximum and minimum of z-scores of each phoneme from native exemplar statistics. All phoneme scores are averaged over each word and then all word scores are aggregated with some weightage given with respect to parts of speech(POS) to get the complete phrase score.

POS	weight	POS	weight	POS	weight
Quantifier	1.0	Adverb	0.8	Possessive	0.6
Noun	0.9	Adjective	0.8	Conjunction	0.5
Verb	0.9	Pronoun	0.7	articles	0.4
Negative	0.8	Preposition	0.6		

Table 3: Weightage of a word based on parts of speech

5.2 Text-independent

The advantage of this Text-independent approach is that we can do pronunciation scoring given any random word or phrase without the requirement of native exemplar recordings for that particular word or phrase. This algorithm is based on pre-determined statistics built from some corpus. Here, in this paper, we used TIMIT corpus to build statistics.

There are 630 speakers in TIMIT each recording 10 sentences. All the wav files are forced-aligned with its transcription to get spectral acoustic match score and duration. Later, we derived statistics for each phone based on its position (begin/middle/end) in the word.

Now, given any random test file, each phone acoustic score, duration is compared with corresponding phone statistics based on its position. The scoring method is same as to that of Text-dependent system.

6 Results

Our main aim of the proposed algorithm is to detect mispronunciations and give reasonable feedback with a score of 1-10. We mainly concentrated on two factors: pronunciation match with correct phone and duration. Edit-distance neighboring phones decoding works well within limits of error-free decoding. Demo of the system is at http://talknicer.net/~ronanki/test/

Initially, we tested the Text-independent system with TIMIT, SA1 and SA2 sentences. The results in Table 4 shows that threshold greater than 7.5 is reasonably good for correct pronunciation. So, we made 7.5 as hard threshold boundary between correct and incorrect pronunciation for any phrase and evaluated the performance of system on our database mentioned in section 3.2. From table 5 and 6, it is observed that Text-independent system works well for phrases even with hard-bounded threshold value.

Sentence	Min.	Max.	Mean	Thres. > 7	Thres. > 7.5	Thres. > 8
SA1	7.14	9.01	8.58	630/630	627/630	612/630
SA2	7.38	8.93	8.50	630/630	627/630	611/630

Table 4: Performance of the TIMIT sentences using Text-independent system

Type	Mean	Thres. > 6	Thres. > 6.5	Thres. > 7
Correct	7.07	354/400	302/400	219/400
Type	Mean	Thres. < 6	Thres. < 6.5	Thres. < 7
Wrong	6.13	170/400	255/400	320/400

Table 5: Performance of words in both cases using Text-independent system

Type	Mean	Thres. > 7	Thres. > 7.5	Thres. > 8
Correct	7.79	108/120	96/120	88/120
Type	Mean	Thres. < 7	Thres. < 7.5	Thres. < 8
Wrong	6.73	86/120	98/120	118/120

Table 6: Performance of sentences in both cases using Text-independent system

Conclusions

Our future work is to concentrate on CART modelling to get better reference statistics based on contextual information of the phone. This tree based clustering model really helps the system to get more efficient scores. Future work will also include deployment on web and stand-alone servers using CMU Sphinx v3 in C, SQL, JavaScript, PHP, Dalvik Java and Objective C. The pronunciation evaluation system really helps second-language learners to improve their pronunciation by trying multiple times and it lets you correct your-self by giving necessary feedback at phone, word level.

References

Chitralekha Bhat, K.L. Srinivas, P. R. (2010). Pronunciation scoring for indian english learners using a phone recognition system. In *Proceedings of the First International Conference on Intelligent Interactive Technologies and Multimedia*, pages 135–139.

Eskenazi, M. (2009). An overview of spoken language technology for education. In *Proc. of Speech Communication, Elsevier, vol 51 issue 10*, pages 832–844.

Eskenazi, M., P. G. (2002). Pinpointing pronunciation errors in children's speech: examining the role of the speech recognizer. In *Proposed to the Pronunciation Modeling and Lexicon Adaptation for Spoken Language Technology Workshop, Sept 2002, Colorado.*

Franco H. Abrash, V. Precoda, K. B. H. R. and J, B. (2000). The sri eduspeak system: Recognition and pronunciation scoring for language learning. In *Proceedings of InSTIL, Scotland*, pages 123–128.

L. Neumeyer, H. Franco, M. W. and Price, P. (1996). Automatic text-independent pronunciation scoring of foreign language student speech. In *Proc. of ICSLP 96, Philadelphia, Pennsylvania*, pages 1457–1460.

Lee, K.-F. (1989). Automatic speech recognition: The development of the sphinx system. In *Kluwer Academic Publishers, Boston.*

Moustroufas, N. and Digalakis, V. (2007). Automatic pronunciation evaluation of foreign speakers using unknown text. In *Comput. Speech Language*, page 219–230.

Peabody, M. A. (2011). *Methods for Pronunciation Assessment in Computer Aided Language Learning.* PhD thesis, Massachusetts Institute of Technology, Cambridge, Massachusetts, USA.

S. Pakhomov, J. Richardson, M. F.-D. and G.Sales (2008). Forced-alignment and edit-distance scoring for vocabulary tutoring applications. In *Lecture Notes in Computer Science, Volume 5246/2008*, pages 443–450.

Seymore, K., C. S. E. S. and R, R. (1996). Language and pronunciation modelling in the cmu 1996 hub-4 evaluation. In *Proc. of DARPA Speech Recognition workshop, chantilly, Virginia, Morgam kaufmann Publishers.*

Sherif Mahdy Abdou, Salah Eldeen Hamid, M. R. A. S. O. A.-H. M. S. and Nazih, W. (2006). Computer aided pronunciation learning system using speech recognition techniques. In *in Interspeech.*

Content Bookmarking and Recommendation

Ananth Vyasarayamut[1] *Satyabrata Behera*[1]
Manideep Attanti[1] *Ganesh Ramakrishnan*[1]
(1) IIT Bombay, India
ananthv@iitb.ac.in, satty@cse.iitb.ac.in, manideep@cse.iitb.ac.in,
ganesh@cse.iitb.ac.in

ABSTRACT
Personalized services are increasingly becoming popular in the Internet. This work proposes a way of generating personalized content and simultaneously recommending users, web pages that, he/she might be interested in, based on his/her personalized content. In this work, we portray a system that not only helps the user in bookmarking the URL and snippets from the web page but also recommends web pages relevant to his/her interest. It applies a content-based filtering approach. We describe the details of the approach and implementation as well as address the challenges associated with it.

KEYWORDS: Bookmarking, Recommendation System, PEBL, Clustering.

1 Introduction

Bookmarking systems allow us to store URLs that we tend to visit often and URLs that had information which were hard to find. As far as we know, there aren't systems which not only store URLs but also store the part of the web page that the user found relevant. For this reason, we need systems which can store this along with the URLs. Still, how do we facilitate others from finding similar content without going through the same hassle? This is where a recommendation system comes into play. This is an attractive feature as it not only gives a greater focus on the content being the principal bookmarked data but also generates recommendations from other users with a similar interest. As an example consider someone buying a telescope. Let's say A is interested in a reasonable aperture telescope but doesn't want it to be too sluggish and has bookmarked a page talking about the Maksutov-Cassegrain telescope. But A might not be aware of the Schmidt-Cassegrain cadioptric scopes which are much lighter and offering a higher aperture too. This could be recommended from a user B who has already made this research and has come across this and has since bookmarked it.
A system was developed using the above approach. This system can be used by a community of people which not only facilitates the recommendation of new web pages to read but also stores the previously read web pages along with the selected text (important parts of web pages) and tags/labels related to the web page entered by the user. The complete approach will be described in the next few sections.

2 Related Work

Recommendation Systems[1] **:** The problem of recommending items has been studied extensively, and two main paradigms have emerged. Content-based recommendation systems try to recommend items, similar to those the user has liked in the past, whereas systems designed according to the collaborative recommendation paradigm identify users whose preferences are similar to those and recommend from those repositories.

For example, a content-based component of the Fab system (Balabanović and Shoham, 1997), which recommends Web pages to users, represents Web page content with the 100 most important words. Similarly, the Syskill & Webert system (Pazzani and Billsus, 1997) represents documents with the 128 most informative words. The "importance" (or "informativeness") of a word in a document is determined with some weighting measure that can be defined in several different ways.
As stated earlier, content-based systems recommend items similar to those that a user has liked in the past. (Lang et al., 1995), (Mooney and Roy, 2000), (Pazzani and Billsus, 1997). In particular, various candidate items are compared with items previously rated by the user and the best-matching item(s) are recommended. They create an user profile for each user depending on the items the user preferred. These profiles are obtained by analyzing the content of the items previously seen and rated by the user and are usually constructed using keyword analysis techniques from information retrieval. All these systems require feedback in the form of ratings from the user. Although our problem is similar to all these mentioned above, the scenario is different in that we do not have pages that the user does not prefer, as in negative instances. Here, only those web pages are bookmarked by the user which he likes. Also the user does not provide any ratings for the web pages. Since we only have web pages that user liked (positive training data), we have more content to learn user interest

[1] referred and extracted from (Adomavicius and Tuzhilin, 2005)

and the disadvantage here, is the unavailability of web pages that the user does not like (negative training data).

GroupLens (Konstan et al., 1997), (Resnick et al., 1994), Video Recommender (Hill et al., 1995), and Ringo (Shardanand and Maes, 1995) were the first systems to use collaborative filtering algorithms to automate prediction. Other examples of collaborative recommendation systems include the book recommendation system from Amazon.com, the PHOAKS system that helps people find relevant information on the WWW (Terveen et al., 1997), and the Jester system that recommends jokes (Goldberg et al., 2001). Since unlike content-based recommendation methods, collaborative recommendation systems (or collaborative filtering systems) try to predict the utility of items for a particular user based on the items previously rated by other users. These scenarios are not related to ours since we only want to recommend web pages related to a user interest and not content from users with similar activity. Also these collaborative systems also require user preference as ratings or likes/dislikes.

Learning from positive examples : Our problem scenario demands learning a model in the absence of negative training data. For this we explored One-Class SVM (Manevitz and Yousef, 2002), PEBL (Positive Example Based Learning for Web Page Classification Using SVM) (Yu et al., 2002) and found that PEBL performs much better than any of the approaches discussed in One-Class SVM. We discuss the implementation and the approach of PEBL in relevant sections.

3 Problem Description

Before stating the problem statement, let's define some terms:
Bookmark : Bookmark consists of two parts : The web page URL and selected text portion of that web page, tags or labels entered by the user reading it. Tags or labels are words that the user wants to store along with the selected text which may capture the basic idea of the web page content or any information relating to the web page.

Content Bookmarking and Recommendation System : This system refers to the process of bookmarking web pages that the user found interesting and is then bookmarked. Each user generates his bookmarks depending on the web pages he browses. Then depending on a user's bookmarks, he is recommended new web pages to read.

Problem Statement : Given a set of users and their bookmarks, the goal is to suggest each user bookmarks, from the bookmarks of other users in that closed community, related/relevant to his existing bookmarks. This can also be interpreted as suggesting a user new web pages to read related to his area of interest (which is indicated by his bookmarks).

This raises the need to create a model for each user capturing the pattern of his bookmarks which necessitates the storage of full text content of each bookmarked web page along with the selected text, tags/labels and URL.

The challenges that were faced and some of which were addressed are listed below:

- It needs to scale well with the addition of users and bookmarks.
- It needs to be fast.
- It should adapt to the change in user's interest indicated by the addition of bookmarks relating new topics.
- It should be time sensitive so that user is suggested more bookmarks related to his current set of interests.

4 Approach

The need to build a model for each user for capturing user interests can be seen in a scenario where a given user has a set of bookmarked web pages which indicates his interest and a set of bookmarked web pages of other users each of which may or may not belong to that given user's interest. This given user's data (i.e. bookmarks) are positive training examples and other user's bookmarks are unlabeled data since it is not known whether they are related to user's interest or not. This reduces to the problem of learning a model where only positive examples are available.

Previous literature was explored for the above and found PEBL(Yu et al., 2002) performs much better than other approaches. So this paper's approach has been implemented to solve our problem. Models are built for each user which captures their interests. These models are used for classifying whether a given web page is relevant to the user or not. Once all the web pages relevant to the user has been found, they are ranked to get the top 'k' web pages. These top 'k' web pages are clustered in order to present the related web pages in groups.

The approach of how the entire system was built is presented below in details :

4.1 PEBL: Positive Example Based Learning for Web Page Classification Using SVM

There is a need to learn a classifier for each user based on their bookmarks. These classifiers are used to classify bookmarks which are relevant to that particular user from the rest of the corpus. On the data, mapping-convergence (M-C) algorithm is run in training phase to build an accurate SVM from positive and unlabeled data. This paper uses SVM since it has properties like maximization of margin, nonlinear transformation of the input space to the feature space using kernel methods and tolerates the problem of high dimensions and sparse instance spaces. These properties makes SVM perform better in many classification domains. The M-C algorithm is as follows:

4.1.1 Mapping Stage

- Identify strong positive features that occurs in the positive training data (POS : bookmarks of a given user) more often than in the unlabeled data (bookmarks of other users).

- By using this list of the positive features, filter out every possible positive data point from the unlabeled data set, which leaves only strongly negative data ($M_1(neg)$). For instance, say a strong negative is a data point not having any of the positive features in the list.

- $S_1(pos)$ denotes unlabeled data points excluding $M_1(neg)$.

4.1.2 Convergence Stage

- This step trains the SVM repeatedly to aggregate mapped negatives ($M_i(neg)$) as close as possible to the unbiased negatives (the bookmarks not relevant to the given user) as per the given user.
- Now add $M_1(neg)$ to the NEG (NEG was empty before this). That is now $NEG = M_1(neg)$.
- Then construct a SVM from the positives (POS) and only the strong negatives $M_1(neg)$,i.e., NEG. The decision hyperplane between POS and NEG would be far from accurate due to the insufficient negative training data. This is shown in figure 1.
- Accumulate $M_2(neg)$ (data points in $S_1(pos)$ which are classified negative by the trained SVM) into NEG, that is, now $NEG = M_1(neg) \bigcup M_2(neg)$.
- Then retrain using POS and NEG.
- Iterate these processes until the $M_i(neg)$ becomes empty set, i.e., when no data in $S_{i-1}(pos)$ is classified as negative. See figure 2.
- The SVM constructed at the end of the process will be close to the SVM constructed from positive and unbiased negative data because NEG will converge into the unbiased negative data in the unlabeled data.

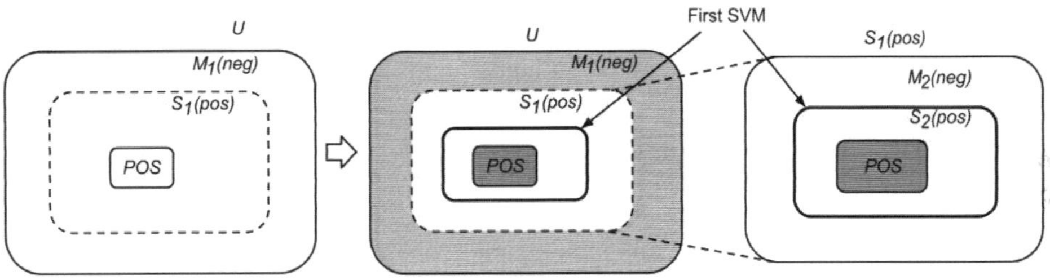

Figure 1: Training first SVM (from $M_1(neg)$ and POS that divides $S_1(pos)$ into $M_2(neg)$ and $S_2(pos)$. Taken from (Yu et al., 2002).

This process is applied to each user to create a SVM classifier for each of them. The SVM classifier of a given user is applied on the bookmarks of other users to find which are relevant to that particular user. The relevant bookmarks/documents are ranked to pick the top 'k' which are highly ranked and fed to the clustering algorithm.

4.2 Ranking Algorithm

Word weights are calculated for each word in the vocabulary considering their occurrence in a given user's bookmarked pages. Then relevant documents for a user are given scores by aggregating weights of the words occurring in them normalized by the length of the

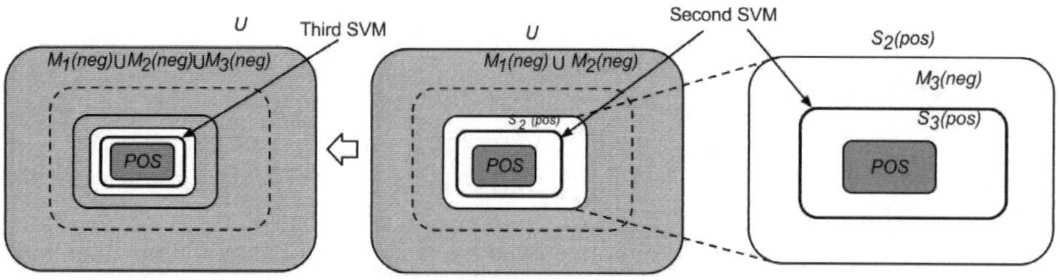

Figure 2: Training second SVM (from $M_1(neg) \bigcup M_2(neg)$and POS that divides $S_2(pos)$ into $M_3(neg)$ and $S_3(pos)$. Taken from (Yu et al., 2002).

document. Then relevant pages are ranked based on their scores and top '*k*' documents are clustered and recommended to the user. All the relevant bookmarks and their scores are stored in the database.

4.3 Clustering Algorithm

Once the relevant bookmarks are found for a user, top k of them are clustered so that related bookmarks are presented as a group. The algorithm used is DBSCAN(Ester et al., 1998). This is chosen because it clusters all documents which are densely distributed in a region and ignores outliers. It doesn't have any constraints of how many clusters have to be formed and also inclusion of every object into some cluster. The choice of minimum similarity between the objects for them to be in a single cluster is obtained by a trial and error method. Also the selection of minimum number of objects around the selected object for it to be the cluster center is done by a trial and error method.

4.4 Feature Design

The bookmarks are preprocessed before determining features and creating feature vector. Pre-processing involves :

- Stop words removal
- Stemming

The stemmed words other than stop words are taken as features. Then each bookmarks is represented as a feature vector whose each column value is the number of times that the word occurred in the document plus a constant multiple of the times it occurs in selected text, tags/labels (constant multiplied to give higher weight to the selected text, tags/labels where this constant multiple is found by trial and error). All the feature vectors are stored in the database. Porter stemmer[2] is used for stemming the words.

4.5 Implementation Specifics

To make the system suitable for a online application, every activity like generating feature vector, training the classifier is done offline. To be clear and precise, when a user bookmarks

[2]http://tartarus.org/ martin/PorterStemmer/def.txt

a web page with selected text, tags/labels, then bookmarked content (web page with selected text, tags/labels) are stored in the database. After storing the bookmark, a module is called to create a feature vector corresponding to those bookmarks using the old features (words, except stop words, that occurred in previous bookmarks that were present when SVM was trained last time). Suppose there are words in the newly added bookmarks which is not there in features, they are kept track of separately. When the size of those new words (new features) crosses a threshold, then feature vectors for all bookmarks are created from scratch w.r.t the updated feature set. Also when a given user adds a bookmarks, that bookmark is tested against his classifier to keep track of change in user's interest. If that is classified as negative, then a counter is incremented to keep track of how many bookmarks added by user is classified wrongly by his classifier. If that number crosses a threshold or if the features set has changed, then retraining of the classifier is done for that user.
Also when a user adds a bookmark, that bookmark is tested against every other user's classifiers to know whether that is relevant to them. If it is, then that bookmark's score is calculated for each of those for whom it is relevant and added to the database table. Then top '*k*' are retrieved and clustered. The clustering information is kept and recommended to the user when logged in.

5 Case Studies

To test the system, user 'A' bookmarked content on Movies and Machine Learning while user 'B' bookmarked content on Cricket and Machine Learning. With a corpus of just over a hundred, the system was able to generate appropriate recommendations. In this case, both A and B got recommendation from web pages pertaining to machine learning. Since recommendations are subjective, a true measure of accuracy cannot be obtained in this system. However, we can 'judge' how well the system worked by getting a measure of the relevance of the documents suggested to the user's corpus. A snapshot of the recommended web pages to user B is shown in figure 3.

The system is able to provide good recommendations. Since all the processing is done

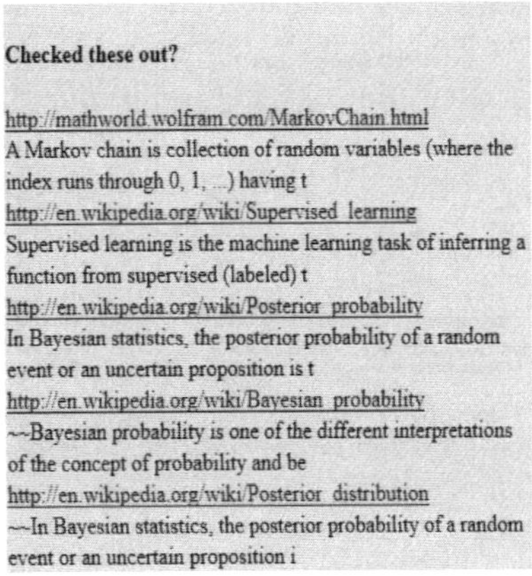

Figure 3: Top 5 relevant results which are recommended to user 'B'

offline (independently - as bookmarks are added to the system, recommendations are calculated and stored in the database table), when user logs in, the recommendations are fetched from the database table and displayed to the user. As described in the previous section, it also takes into account change in user interest.

6 Conclusion

The system designed here, for content bookmarking and recommendation can be used where the user's intention is to not only bookmark the URL but specific part of the web page that is relevant. Each bookmark can also be tagged, if necessary by the user. This system also generates recommendations based on the user's interest and is implemented in a generic manner so as to not adhere to any specific domain.
The usage of PEBL enables us to get a reasonably good accuracy and although our data does not entirely validate this, we still believe it is capable of further fine grained classification. In the future work, we expect to add the property of time sensitivity so that the current interests of the user are given more priority while providing recommendations.

References

Adomavicius, G. and Tuzhilin, A. (2005). Toward the next generation of recommender systems: A survey of the state-of-the-art and possible extensions. *Knowledge and Data Engineering, IEEE Transactions on*, 17(6):734–749.

Balabanović, M. and Shoham, Y. (1997). Fab: content-based, collaborative recommendation. *Communications of the ACM*, 40(3):66–72.

Ester, M., Kriegel, H., Sander, J., Wimmer, M., and Xu, X. (1998). Incremental clustering for mining in a data warehousing environment. In *Proceedings of the International Conference on Very Large Data Bases*, pages 323–333. Institute Of Electrical & Electronics Engineers.

Goldberg, K., Roeder, T., Gupta, D., and Perkins, C. (2001). Eigentaste: A constant time collaborative filtering algorithm. *Information Retrieval*, 4(2):133–151.

Hill, W., Stead, L., Rosenstein, M., and Furnas, G. (1995). Recommending and evaluating choices in a virtual community of use. In *Proceedings of the SIGCHI conference on Human factors in computing systems*, pages 194–201. ACM Press/Addison-Wesley Publishing Co.

Konstan, J., Miller, B., Maltz, D., Herlocker, J., Gordon, L., and Riedl, J. (1997). Grouplens: applying collaborative filtering to usenet news. *Communications of the ACM*, 40(3):77–87.

Lang, K. et al. (1995). News weeder: Learning to filter netnews. In *Proc. International Conference on Machine Learning*, pages 331–339. Morgan Kaufmann Publishers, Inc.

Manevitz, L. and Yousef, M. (2002). One-class svms for document classification. *the Journal of machine Learning research*, 2:139–154.

Mooney, R. and Roy, L. (2000). Content-based book recommending using learning for text categorization. In *Proceedings of the fifth ACM conference on Digital libraries*, pages 195–204. ACM.

Pazzani, M. and Billsus, D. (1997). Learning and revising user profiles: The identification of interesting web sites. *Machine learning*, 27(3):313–331.

Resnick, P., Iacovou, N., Suchak, M., Bergstrom, P., and Riedl, J. (1994). Grouplens: an open architecture for collaborative filtering of netnews. In *Proceedings of the 1994 ACM conference on Computer supported cooperative work*, pages 175–186. ACM.

Shardanand, U. and Maes, P. (1995). Social information filtering: algorithms for automating "word of mouth". In *Proceedings of the SIGCHI conference on Human factors in computing systems*, pages 210–217. ACM Press/Addison-Wesley Publishing Co.

Terveen, L., Hill, W., Amento, B., McDonald, D., and Creter, J. (1997). Phoaks: A system for sharing recommendations. *Communications of the ACM*, 40(3):59–62.

Yu, H., Han, J., and Chang, K. (2002). Pebl: positive example based learning for web page classification using svm. In *Proceedings of the eighth ACM SIGKDD international conference on Knowledge discovery and data mining*, pages 239–248. ACM.

A template matching approach for detecting pronunciation mismatch

Lavanya Prahallad, Radhika Mamidi, Kishore Prahallad
International Institute of Information Technology, Hyderabad, India.
{lavanya@research, radhika.mamidi, kishore}@iiit.ac.in

ABSTRACT
In this paper, we study the usefulness of the best path and the complete trellis in dynamic programming based template matching approach for detecting pronunciation mismatch. We show that there exists cues in trellis (a matrix representing all paths), which could be exploited for detecting pronunciation mismatch. Such an approach could be used to build a template based approach for detecting pronunciation mismatch independent of the language.

KEYWORDS: Pronunciation mismatch, dynamic programming, template matching.

KEYWORDS IN L_2: .

1 Template based approach

Detection of pronunciation mismatch plays a crucial role in the computer-assisted pronunciation training (CAPT). A CAPT system is built using an automatic speech recognition system (Delmonte, 2000) (Ehsani and Knodt, 1998) (Eskenazi, 2009) (Stenson et al., 1992). A template matching algorithm provides greater flexibility than a model-based (such as hidden Markov models) approach in building an automated tutor for second language learning and acquisition. Model-based approaches are resource intensive. It needs a lot more speech data than single templates or exemplars to build acoustic models of the native and non-native speakers. In the case of template based approaches, a single reference template is deemed sufficient. Template based approaches could also be scaled to a new language easily.

Amongst template matching algorithms, dynamic programming is mostly commonly used as it performs nonlinear alignment of test and reference patterns. The best path aligning the test and reference templates is chosen using the Viterbi algorithm. The cost of this alignment is typically subjected to a threshold to detect pronunciation mismatch in the test and reference templates. The cost of the alignment depends on several factors including the recording environment, speaker/learner, and the amount of pronunciation mismatch in the test template. Thus, the alignment cost is subjected to some form of normalization (what type of normalization etc., give references). Inspite of normalization of scores, it is not easy to detect subtle pronunciation variations in the template based approaches. For example, in English, it is hard to detect /sh/ when it is replaced with /s/ using a template based approach.

In this paper, we show that it is important to look at the cues present in the scores of the entire trellis than computing the best path. A trellis is a matrix representing all the possible alignment paths between the test and reference templates. The best path computation using the Viterbi algorithm is designed to optimise the score between the test and reference template. Thus, we argue that it is better to delay the process of computing the best path, and focus on the scores along the diagonal of the trellis.

In order to demonstrate the usefulness of the cues in the trellis we make use of synthetic speech, i.e., speech generated by a text-to-speech system. A good text-to-speech (TTS) system faithfully generates a waveform corresponding to the text input or to a sequence of phonemes. A TTS system is usually built using a single speaker's voice. Thus a test or reference example generated by a TTS will have the same speaker's voice. Thus the variability in the speaker characteristics is suppressed. This acts as an advantage to our study to show that the cues in the trellis highlight the subtle pronunciation mismatches in the test and reference templates.

This paper is organized as follows. Section 2 discusses the synthetic data used in this work. Section 3 explains the significance of trellis in highlighting the mismatches. Section 4 discusses the results.

2 Synthesized speech data set

To generate synthesized speech data, we have used US KAL diphone voice in festival speech synthesis system. A diphone voice is unit selection voice, where the required set of diphones are collected from the speaker, these diphones are modified in terms of duration and intonation based on the context. A smooth concatenation of these prosodically modified diphones is done to generate a synthetic speech. In this work, we have generated 10 synthesized words with correct and incorrect pronunciation. The correct pronunciation of a word is automatically generated by pronunciation lexicon in the festival speech synthesis system, to generate incorrect

Word	Correct Pron.	Incorrect Pron.
sugar	sh uh g er	s uh g er
gym	jh ih m	jh ay m
honey	hh ah n iy	hh aa n ey
though	dh ow	dh ao
daughter	d ao t er	d aa t er
zero	z ih r ow	jh ih r ao
snack	s n ae k	s n aa k
honor	aa n er	aa n er
caught	k aa t	k aa t
eight	ey t	ay t ey

Table 1: List of words with correct and incorrect pronunciation

pronunciation we have manually identified a sequence of phonemes for each word, where there is at least one incorrect phoneme. Table 1 shows the set of 10 words, their correct and incorrect pronunciation.

3 Alignment using dynamic programming

Given that we have generated synthetic speech data with correct and incorrect pronunciation, we now describe the features extracted and the dynamic programming based alignment in the below sections:

3.1 Feature extraction

The speech signal is processed to generate linear prediction cepstral coefficients (LPCCs). These features are generated for every block of 10 milli seconds using a frame shift of 5 milli seconds. For each frame a 12th order linear prediction analysis is applied to extract 17 dimension LPCCs.

3.2 Forward algorithm

Let $Y = \{\boldsymbol{y}(1), \boldsymbol{y}(2), \ldots, \boldsymbol{y}(T)\}$ be a sequence of observed feature vectors for the correct pronunciation. Let $X = \{\boldsymbol{x}(1), \boldsymbol{x}(2), \ldots, \boldsymbol{x}(M)\}$ be a sequence of observed feature vectors for the incorrect pronunciation. The dynamic programming aligns the feature vectors Y with X. The result is stretched or shrunk signal $X' = \{\boldsymbol{x}(1), \boldsymbol{x}(2), \ldots, \boldsymbol{x}(T)\}$. The dynamic programming algorithm to compute X' is as explained below. This is explained in the probability-like domain, as apposed to tradition Euclidean distance domain.

Let $1 \leq j \leq M$, $1 \leq i \leq M$, and $1 \leq t \leq T$. Let us define $\alpha_t(j)$ as a cost or score incurred to align j^{th} feature of X with t^{th} feature vector of Y.

The $\alpha_t(j)$ could be computed frame-by-frame using the recursive Viterbi equation

$$\alpha_t(j) = \max_i \{\alpha_{t-1}(i) a_{i,j}\} P(\boldsymbol{y}(t), \boldsymbol{x}(j)), \tag{1}$$

where $P(\boldsymbol{y}(t), \boldsymbol{x}(j)) = exp(\|\boldsymbol{y}(t) - \boldsymbol{x}(j)\|^2)$, and $\|.\|^2$ represents the Euclidean distance between two feature vectors. Here $i = \{j, j-1, j-2\}$. The value of $a_{i,j} = 1$, thus making all paths (including non-diagonal) leading from $(i, t-1)$ to (j, t) are given uniform weightage.

The value $P(\mathbf{y}(t), \mathbf{x}(j))$ is typically less than 1. For large values of t, $\alpha_t(.)$ tends exponentially to zero, and its computation exceeds the precision range of any machine (Rabiner and Juang, 1993). Hence $\alpha_t(.)$ is scaled with term $\frac{1}{\max\limits_i\{\alpha_t(i)\}}$, at every time instant t. This normalization ensures that values of $\alpha_t(.)$ are between 0 and 1 at time t.

Given $\alpha_t(.)$, a backtracking algorithm is used to find the best alignment path. In order to backtrack, an addition variable ϕ is used to store the path as follows.

$$\phi_t(j) = \operatorname*{argmax}_i \{\alpha_{t-1}(i) a_{i,j}\}, \tag{2}$$

where $\phi_t(j)$ denotes the frame number (index of the feature vector) at time $(t-1)$ which provides an optimal path to reach state j at time t.

3.3 Best path

Given values of $\phi_t(.)$, a typical backtracking done to obtain the best path is as follows:

$$y(T) = N \tag{3}$$
$$y(t) = \phi_{t+1}(y(t+1)),\ t = T-1, T-2, \ldots, 1. \tag{4}$$

4 Results and discussion

4.1 Best path Vs. Full trellis

Any typical template matching algorithm works with the best path. It has to be noted that the best path is one of the paths in the entire trellis. Our argument is that there exists cues in the trellis about the weak alignment spots, which are not clearly indicated in the best path. In order to demonstrate it, we align the utterances corresponding to /s uh g er/ (incorrect pronunciation) and /sh uh g er/ (correct pronunciation) using dynamic programming. Fig. 1(a) shows the best path of this alignment, i.e., $y(t)$ for $t = 1 \ldots T$, as defined in Eq. (4). Fig. 1(b) shows the complete trellis, i.e, $\alpha_t j$ for all values of t and j. It could be observed that the best path in Fig. 1(a) does not highlight or show explicitly any type of mismatch between the aligned utterances. Fig. 1(b) highlights that there is a weak spot (a set of white pixels denoting a white patch) along the diagonal. The time stamps of this weak spot correspond to alignment of /sh/ with /s/. Thus the full trellis could be useful is detecting a pronunciation mismatch. Using a simple algorithm, we have automatically detected this weak spot, and is as shown in Fig. 1(c).

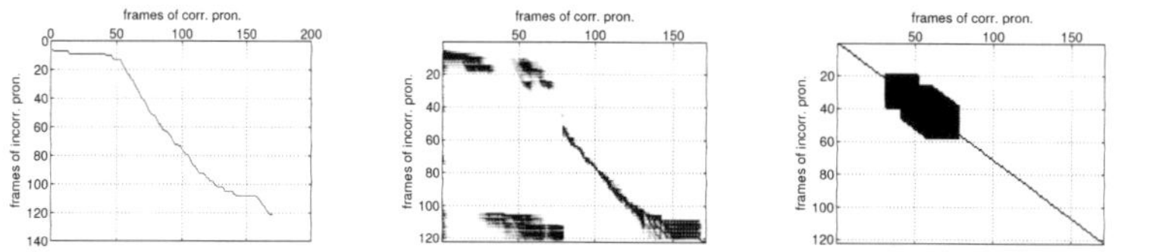

(a) Best path (b) Complete trellis (c) Automatically detected weak spots in the trellis

Figure 1: Alignment of /s uh g er/ with /sh uh g er/.

Fig. 2 provides the similar results for the rest of the utterances.

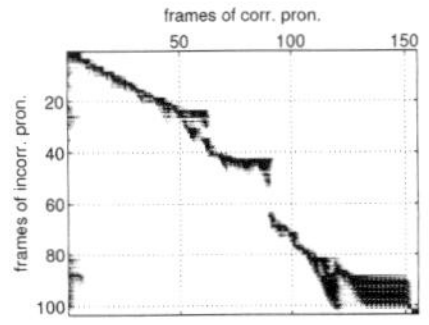

(a) /jh ay m/ Vs /jh ih m/

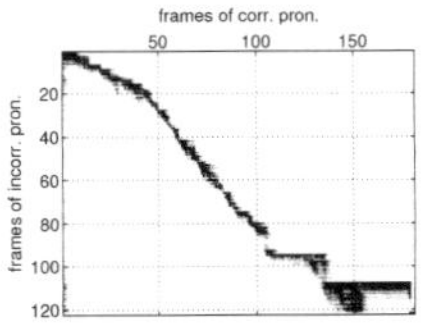

(b) /hh aa n ey/ Vs /hh ah n iy/

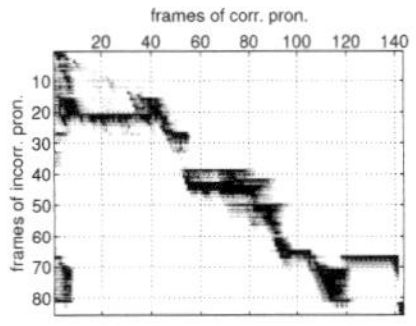

(c) /dh ao/ Vs /dh ow/

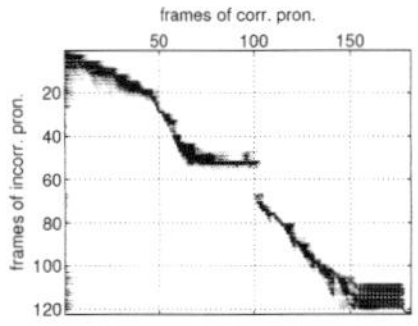

(d) /d aa t er/ Vs /d ao t er/

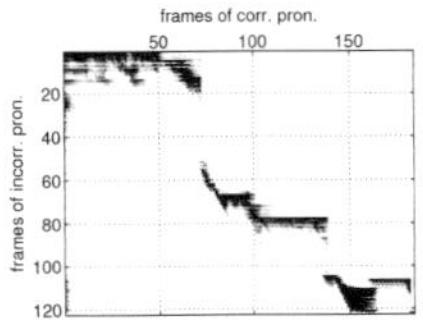

(e) /jh ih r ao/ Vs /z ih r ow/

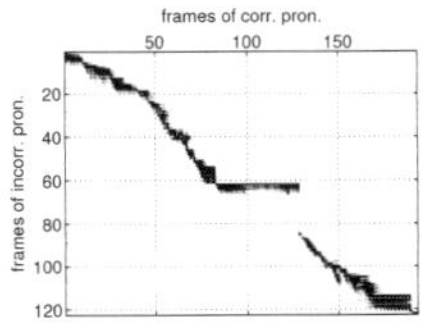

(f) /s n aa k/ Vs /s n ae k/

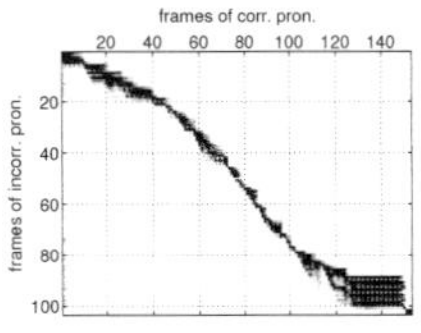

(g) /aa n er/ Vs /aa n er/

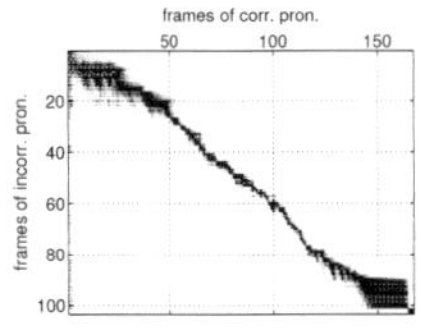

(h) /k aa t/ Vs /k aa t/

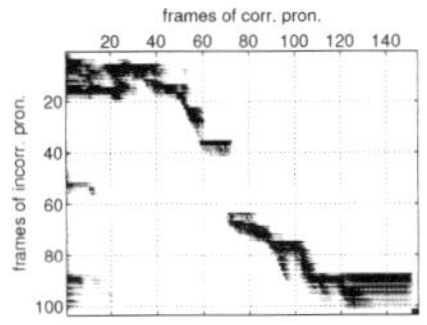

(i) /ay t ey/ Vs /ey t/

Figure 2: Trellis of the dynamic programming alignments

5 Conclusions

In this paper, we have demonstrated the usefulness of complete trellis in a template matching approach for detecting pronunciation mismatch. We have shown that the complete trellis provide more cues than using the best path, as done traditionally. The experiments in this paper are done using synthetic speech samples. We plan to investigate the usefulness of the trellis on real data sets, and build a pronunciation learning system using template based approach.

A major question is whether such cues are present in real datasets involving two speakers. Our informal experiments show that such cues exists. Moreover, our approach of building a pronunciation learning system is to have the learner imitate a teacher or a reference template. One could use thresholds suiting to a requirement of a strict or a lenient system during automatic detection of weak spots in the trellis.

References

Delmonte, R. (2000). Slim prosodic automatic tools for self-learning instruction. *Speech Communication*, 30(2–3):145 – 166.

Ehsani, F. and Knodt, E. (1998). Speech technology in computer-aided language learning: Strengths and limitations of a new call paradigm. *Language Learning and Technology*, 2(1):45–60.

Eskenazi, M. (2009). An overview of spoken language technology for education. *Speech Communication*, 51(1):832–844.

Rabiner, L. R. and Juang, B. H. (1993). *Fundamentals of Speech Recognition*. Prentice-Hall.

Stenson, N. et al. (1992). The effectiveness of computer-assisted pronunciation training. *Calico Journal*, 9(4):5–19.

Automatic Easy Japanese Translation for information accessibility of foreigners

Manami MOKU [1] *Kazuhide YAMAMOTO* [1] *Ai MAKABI* [1]
(1) Department of Electrical Engineering, Nagaoka University of Technology,
1603-1, Kamitomioka-cho, Nagaoka-city, Niigata 940-2188, JAPAN
{moku, yamamoto, makabi}@jnlp.org

ABSTRACT

This paper examines the introduction of "Easy Japanese" by extracting important segments for translation. The need for Japanese language has increased dramatically due to the recent influx of non-Japanese-speaking foreigners. Therefore, in order for non-native speakers of Japanese to successfully adapt to society, the so-called Easy Japanese is being developed to aid them in every aspect from basic conversation to translation of official documents. The materials of our project are the official documents since they are generally distributed in public offices, hospitals, and schools, where they include essential information that should be accessed for all residents. Through an analysis of Japanese language dependency as a pre-experiment, this paper introduces a translation by extracting important segments to facilitate the acquisition of Easy Japanese. Upon effective completion, the project will be introduced for use on the Internet and proposed for use by foreigners living in Japan as well as educators.

KEYWORDS : Easy Japanese, Extracting important segments, Translation system, Official documents, Japanese education.

1 Introduction

It is estimated that more than two million foreigners are now living in Japan and roughly a half million of those do not have enough Japanese fluency. Since only Japanese is used in ordinary Japanese society, it has been a problem in Japan in terms of information accessibility to such foreigners.

One solution for this is use of simple and plain expressions for communication to those. Several trials have been attempted to define and spread somewhat simple expressions to the non-Japanese community, mainly by Japanese language teachers. We are joining "Easy Japanese" project (Isao Iori, 2008) since last year. Although it is also a project to teach easy Japanese to foreigners, one goal of this project is to automatically "translate" (or summarize easily) ordinary Japanese sentences into easy one, by use of natural language processing (NLP) techniques. The target material of the project is official documents that are generally distributed in public offices, hospitals, and schools, where they include essential information that should be accessed for all residents.

It is observed that official documents may include some peculiar expressions that make it difficult for foreigners to understand. For example, in case of English, we may see something like: "Please avoid your children's attendance in school with an assessment of the situation by a guardian when the situation is dangerous for children in case of bad weather." Although it is no problem to understand for native speakers, it is far easier for non-native speakers just to say like: "Don't go to school in case of bad weather." We aim to build a system to translate a sentence like the former one into the latter one. We propose in this paper to do that by extracting essential segments and rewriting them into more direct expressions. This paper briefly reports outline of the project, approach of the current translation system, and results of preliminary experiments.

2 Related works

2.1 Easy Japanese

This system of so-called Easy Japanese has been previously researched by those in the translation of news. In one particular study, easy and difficult words from the news were defined (Hideya Mino et al., 2010). In this case, the authors utilized pairs of entities, and the word levels were defined on the basis of a word list from the Japanese Language Proficiency Test (JLPT).[1] This method was general method since there were similar methods.

2.1.1 Easy Japanese system

A previous Easy Japanese system, known as the Plain Japanese (PJ) system,[2] was designed for use in engineering education in Japan. Although such education is generally in Japanese, international students find it difficult not only to learn everyday Japanese but also acquire technical Japanese. In this case, this system used both restricted vocabulary and grammar. Therefore, this method was not suitable for our system since we aim to extract such important contents.

---

[1] http://www.jlpt.jp/e/index.html : This site is written in English.
JLPT is one of tests for Japanese beginners who learn Japanese. This research use the grade of JLPT, N1~N5.
[2] http://twinning.nagaokaut.ac.jp/PJ/PJ.html : This site is written in Japanese.

2.2 Extraction of important contents

Extracting important contents and sentences (Tsutomu Hirano et al., 2005) was generally used for summarization since the summary maintains natural grammar. However, sometimes, abstract sentences are reconstructed from some natural sentences. In one particular study, important segments were extracted for summaries using Support Vector Machines (SVMs) (Daisuke Suzuki et al., 2006), which was more effective when summarizing documents compared to extracting important sentences. We believe that extracting important segments can be the same as talking with Japanese language beginners. Therefore, we would like to re-introduce an easy process based on Japanese dependency analysis since we do not have more examples of important segment extraction in official documents using SVMs.

3 Data

3.1 Easy Japanese corpus

Easy Japanese overall includes two corpora. The first Easy Japanese pre-corpus was created by two Japanese teachers (Chie Tsutsui, 2010) and included 1,179 sentences from official documents that were rewritten into Easy Japanese. In this case, "easy" implies that Japanese language beginners can easily understand words/sentences, whereas "difficult" indicates that they simply cannot understand the sentences. For this first corpus, the grammar was considered by our project member while the vocabulary was determined on the basis of Japanese Language Proficiency Test (JLPT) levels.

The second Easy Japanese corpus was created by 40 Japanese teachers and it included 42,274 official sentences that were rewritten into Easy Japanese. An example of these language pairs is shown in TABLE 1.

For this paper, Easy Japanese pre-corpus is used for evaluating and extracting important segments. In addition, the Easy Japanese corpus will be used for building the Easy Japanese translation system.

<table>
<tr><th colspan="2"></th><th colspan="2">Kind of corpus</th><th>Japanese</th><th>English</th></tr>
<tr><td rowspan="3">output</td><td>Japanese</td><td rowspan="2">Easy Japanese Pre-corpus</td><td rowspan="3">Easy Japanese Corpus</td><td>予防接種</td><td>a vaccination</td></tr>
<tr><td rowspan="2">Easy Japanese</td><td>予防注射</td><td>a preventive injection</td></tr>
<tr><td></td><td>病気にならないための注射</td><td>an injection which prevents a disease</td></tr>
</table>

TABLE 1 - An example of a pair of Japanese and Easy Japanese from each corpora.

4 Pre-experiment for extracting important segments

4.1 Important segment extraction

First, we focused on the predicates of official sentences since the important contents, especially the instructions, were constructed with verbs. In addition, we randomly selected 20 sentences from the Easy Japanese pre-corpus, and the sentences were edited with conjunctions and keywords such as "場合 (in case of)" through morphological analysis by ChaSen.[3] An example is shown in TABLE 2.

Next, the sentences were analyzed through a Japanese dependency analysis by CaboCha,[4] and the output of this process became the candidates for these important sentences. An example is shown in TABLE 3.

		Japanese	English
input		悪天候の際には，大雨警報，暴風警報，大雪警報，暴風雪警報が発令されていなくても，周囲の状況で危険な場合は，保護者の判断で登校を見合わせてください.	Please avoid your children's attendance in school with an assessment of the situation by a guardian when the situation is dangerous for children and no warning is issued in case of bad weather.
output	I	悪天候の際には，	in case of bad weather
	II	大雨警報，暴風警報，大雪警報，暴風雪警報が発令されていなくても，周囲の状況で危険な場合は，	when the situation is dangerous for children and no warning is issued
	III	保護者の判断で登校を見合わせてください.	Please avoid your children's attendance in school with an assessment of the situation by a guardian

TABLE 2 - An example of the process for decreasing errors in the Japanese dependency analysis.

		Japanese	English
input		保護者の判断で登校を見合わせてください.	Please avoid your children's attendance in school with an assessment of the situation by a guardian.
Japanese dependency analysis		保護者の –D 判断で –D 登校を –D 見合わせてください.	by a guardian with an assessment of the situation your children's attendance in school Please avoid
output	I	保護者の判断で見合わせてください.	Please avoid with an assessment of the situation by a guardian.
	II	登校を見合わせてください.	Please avoid your children's attendance in school.

TABLE 3 - An example of Japanese dependency analysis.

---

[3] Morphological Analysis, ChaSen, Ver.2.3.3,
Nara Institute of Science and Technology, Computational Linguistics Laboratory
http://chasen.naist.jp/hiki/ChaSen/,
[4] Japanese dependency analysis, CaboCha
Nara Institute of Science and Technology, Taku Kudo
http://code.ge.g.,oogle.com/p/cabocha/

		Japanese	English
output	I	保護者の判断で見合わせてください．	Please avoid with an assessment of the situation by a guardian.
	II	登校を見合わせてください．	Please avoid your children's attendance to school.

TABLE 4 - An example of output selection.

Finally, we selected the final output from these candidates and focused on postpositional words, especially with regard to particles attached with nouns for easy judgment. In addition, we established an order of priority for the particles. An example is shown in TABLE 4. In the case of example "登校を見合わせてください (Please avoid your children's attendance to school)", this phrase was selected as the system's output.

4.2 Rewriting into direct expressions

The outputs, after extracting the important segments, were shorter than the original sentences. However, it was still difficult for Japanese language beginners to read them. Therefore, we rewrote 165 sentences into direct expressions that could be easily utilized by these beginners, which included pairs of official segments and segments of direct expressions similar to TABLE 1.

5 Evaluating pre-experiments

The Easy Japanese expressions were not only understandable for Japanese language beginners but also native Japanese speakers. Consequently, the outputs were evaluated by one of the authors of this project, who is a native speaker of Japanese.

5.1 Data for evaluation

We randomly extracted 20 sentences from the Easy Japanese pre-corpus and analyzed them for the extraction processes. An example is shown in TABLE 5. The method of evaluation included a two-tiered process that compared the input and output sentences.

		Japanese	English
input		手続きには，診断書はいりません．所定の用紙がありますので，該当するようなけがをした場合は，担任または顧問まですぐにお知らせください．	You don't need a medical certificate for a processing. Please tell your homeroom teacher or an advisor about your injury with the prescribed form, which follows the rules of our school.
output	I	診断書はいりません．	You don't need a medical certificate.
	II	所定の用紙があります．	There is a prescribed form.
	III	該当するようなけがをした場合は，	When your injury follows the rules of our school
	IV	お知らせください．	Please tell us about it.

TABLE 5 - An example of evaluation data.

First, the process included extracting important sentences (9.1), which was ineffective according to the results due to the order of priority for the particles. In this case, the particles depend upon each of the verbs. Therefore, it was necessary to consider the particles of each verb because the verbs in data alone were insufficient for obtaining the particles.

Next, the process included rewriting the sentences into direct expressions (9.2), which was also ineffective since the pairs were insufficient for obtaining a significant result. However, we found that the pairs of Japanese and Easy Japanese included many points of similarity. In future research, we will utilize existing pairs of Japanese and Easy Japanese (Manami Moku et al., 2011) or create new pairs from them.

Conclusion and perspectives

When extracting important segments, we considered that predicates included important information and particles were defined by the order of priority. However, the particles relied upon each of the verbs. We believe that our findings will be important for Japanese language beginners, and the Easy Japanese corpus will be utilized for future experiments since the corpus is smaller.

In addition, after rewriting the sentences into direct expressions, we found that the direct expressions had many similarities to Easy Japanese. Furthermore, we will use the pairs of Japanese and Easy Japanese for it.

Finally, in regard to the Easy Japanese system, the system will include three overall steps: (1) Extract important segments; (2) Create tags for representation of intention; and (3) Rewrite Japanese into Easy Japanese. Furthermore, we understand that the direct expressions include many similarities to Easy Japanese. Consequently, we will utilize data comprising pairs of Japanese and easy Japanese sentences for our project, and through the processes, we will create a system that can be used on the Internet by Japanese language beginners.

References

Chie Tsutsui. (2010). Creation of pre-corpus, *The Meeting of Society for Teaching Japanese as a Foreign Language in 2009*, The Spring Meeting in 2009, pages 86 –87

Daisuke Suzuki and Akira Utaumi. (2006). A Method for Extracting Important Segments from Documents Using Support Vector Machines: Toward Automatic Text Summarization, The Japanese Society for Artificial Intelligence, vol.21, no.4, B, pages 330–339

Isao Iori. (2008). Surround Easy Japanese, *The 4th Society to Study for Teaching Japanese as a Foreign Language in Multicultural Symbolical Society*, pages 1–12

Hideya Mino and Hideki Tanaka. (2010). Simplifying noun using Japanese dictionary in news, *The 16th Yearly Meeting of Association for Natural Language Processing*, pages 760–763

Manami Moku and Kazuhide Yamamoto. (2011). Investigation of Paraphrase of Easy Japanese in Official Documents, *The 17th Yearly Meeting of Association for Natural Language Processing*, pages 376–379

Tsutomu Hirano, Hideki Isozaki, Eisaku Maeda and Yuji Matsumoto. (2002). Extracting Important Sentences with Support Vector Machines, *Proceedings of the 19th International Conference on Computational Linguistics (COLING 2002)*, pp.342–348

Genre–oriented Readability Assessment: a Case Study

Felice Dell'Orletta Giulia Venturi Simonetta Montemagni
Istituto di Linguistica Computazionale "Antonio Zampolli" (ILC–CNR), via G. Moruzzi, 1 – Pisa (Italy)
{felice.dellorletta,giulia.venturi,simonetta.montemagni}@ilc.cnr.it

ABSTRACT
Whether and to what extent readability assessment is genre–dependent is an issue which has important consequences also in the design and development of educational applications. In this paper, we address this issue from an applicative point of view by investigating whether general purpose readability assessment tools can reliably be used for dealing with texts belonging to different genres. Different experiments have been carried out showing that classification–based approaches to readability assessment can achieve reliable results only by using genre–specific models. Since the construction of genre–specific models is a time consuming task, we proposed a new ranking method for readability assessment based on the notion of distance: we also showed that this method can be usefully exploited for automatically building genre–specific training corpora, thus creating the prerequisites for overcoming the inherent problems of classification–based readability assessment. All reported experiments have been carried out on Italian, a less—resourced language as far as readability assessment is concerned.

Valutazione della Leggibilità e Generi Testuali: un Caso di Studio

Se e in che misura la valutazione della leggibilità sia influenzata dal genere testuale rappresenta una questione che ha importanti conseguenze anche al livello dello sviluppo di applicazioni in ambito didattico. In questo contributo, affrontiamo questo problema da una prospettiva applicativa, verificando se strumenti per il calcolo della leggibilità sviluppati per un uso generale siano affidabili quando applicati a testi appartenenti a diversi generi testuali. Sono stati condotti diversi esperimenti che hanno mostrato che approcci al calcolo della leggibilità basati sul metodo della classificazione possono restituire risultati affidabili solo se utilizzano modelli specifici per ogni genere. Dal momento che la costruzione di tali modelli specifici è un compito impegnativo, abbiamo proposto un nuovo metodo di ranking per il calcolo della leggibilità basato sulla nozione di distanza che può essere utilizzato anche per la costruzione automatica di corpora di addestramento specifici di genere. Tutti gli esperimenti riportati sono stati condotti sull'italiano, lingua per la quale sono a disposizione poche risorse.

KEYWORDS: Readability Assessment, Textual Genre, Automatic Construction of Corpora, Less–resourced Languages.

KEYWORDS IN L_2: Calcolo della Leggibilità, Generi Testuali, Costruzione Automatica di Corpora, Lingue con Poche Risorse.

1 Introduction

Over the last ten years, the development of efficient natural language processing (NLP) systems led to a resurgence of interest in readability assessment. Several studies have been carried out based on NLP-enabled feature extraction and state–of–the–art machine learning algorithms with significant performance improvement with respect to traditional readability measures. Due to the great potential of automatic readability assessment for educational purposes, many of these studies, mostly focused on English but also tackling less–resourced languages, have been carried out with the final aim of supporting teachers and/or learners in selecting material which is appropriate to a given reading level. In principle, educational material can belong to different textual genres, ranging e.g. from fiction to scientific writing or reportage. The question which naturally arises is whether and to what extent readability assessment is genre–independent, and if this not the case whether and how general purpose readability assessment tools could reliably be used for dealing with texts belonging to different genres. The most recent literature on readability reports that the degree of readability is connected to genre: consider, for instance, the work by (Kate et al., 2010) who improves the accuracy of readability predictions by using genre–specific features, or by (Štajner et al., 2012) who proved that linguistic features correlated with readability are also genre dependent. This suggests that textual genre and readability do not represent orthogonal dimensions of classification, but intertwined notions whose complex interplay needs to be further investigated in order to envisage solutions which could be successfully exploited in real educational applications.

NLP–based approaches to readability assessment proposed in the literature can be subdivided into two groups, according to whether readability assessment is carried out as a classification task (see among others (Petersen and Ostendorf, 2009; Aluisio et al., 2010; Feng et al., 2010; Nenkova et al., 2010; Dell'Orletta et al., 2011b)) or in terms of ranking (see, among others, (Tanaka-Ishii et al., 2010),(Ma et al., 2012), (Inui and Yamamoto, 2001)). Methods following a classification approach carry out this task by assigning the document under analysis to a specific readability class, while ranking–based methods assign the document a score positioning it within a readability ranking scale. From this it follows that whereas a classification–based system requires a predefined set of classes of readability, ranking methods do not assume any readability leveling system besides the extreme poles representing maximum and minimum readability. The main problem of classification–based methods is represented by the lack of training data representative of fine-grained readability classes: it goes without saying that this is even more problematic for less–resourced languages. Moreover, if it turns out to be true that the notion of readability has to be tailored with respect to textual genres, such resources would in principle be needed for each genre: this represents an unrealistic goal. Ranking–based readability assessment methods represent a viable alternative to classification methods, since they only require training data with respect to two readability levels (easy vs difficult).

The work reported in this paper is aimed at shedding light on the complex interplay between genre and readability analysis, with the goal of exploring workable solutions which might be exploited in real–world educational applications. This goal was pursued in two different steps. Firstly, we demonstrated that readability assessment is genre–dependent: we carried out two classification–based readability assessment experiments and compared the results achieved in classifying documents which belong to different genres using a single readability model and genre–specific models. Secondly, we proposed a new ranking–based readability assessment method exploiting complex linguistic features identified within the output of NLP tools. All reported experiments have been carried out on a less–resourced language, i.e. Italian.

2 Corpora and Tools

For the specific concerns of this study, we focused on four traditional textual genres: Journalism, Literature, Educational writing and Scientific prose. Each genre was further subdivided in two classes according to their expected target audience, taken as indicative of the accessibility level of the document. The journalistic genre class includes two different corpora: a newspaper corpus, *La Repubblica*, and an easy–to–read newspaper, *Due Parole* which was specifically written by linguists expert in text simplification using a controlled language for an audience of adults with a rudimentary literacy level or with mild intellectual disabilities (Piemontese, 1996). The Literature and Educational genre classes are partitioned into two subclasses, including texts respectively targeting children vs adults. The scientific prose genre class includes articles from Wikipedia as opposed to scientific articles. Among all these corpora, due to its peculiar nature *Due Parole* is to be considered as the easiest–to–read corpus. Corpora selected as representative of the different genre classes and accessibility levels are detailed in Table 1.

For the experiments reported below, each corpus representative of a fine–grained subclass, corresponding to a textual genre and targeting a specific audience, was split into training and test sets. Each test set consists of 30 selected documents, whereas the training sets include the remaining documents, namely: 292 (2Par), 291 (Rep), 71 (ChildLit), 297 (AdLit), 97 (ChildEdu), 40 (AdEdu), 263 (Wiki) and 54 (ScientArt). These corpora were automatically POS tagged by the Part–Of–Speech tagger described in (Dell'Orletta, 2009) and dependency–parsed by the DeSR parser (Attardi, 2006) using Support Vector Machine as learning algorithm.

For readability classification experiments we used READ–IT (Dell'Orletta et al., 2011b), the only available NLP–based readability assessment tool dealing with Italian texts. It uses lexical, morpho–syntactic and syntactic features, listed in Table 2, which are reliably identified from syntactically (i.e. dependency) parsed texts. It is a classifier based on Support Vector Machines that, given a set of features and a training corpus, creates a statistical model which is used in the assessment of readability of unseen documents.

Abbreviation name	Corpus	Coarse–grained genre	N.documents	N.words
Rep	*La Repubblica* (Marinelli et al., 2003), Italian newspaper	*Journalism*	321	232,908
2Par	*Due Parole*, easy–to–read Italian newspaper (Piemontese, 1996)	*Journalism*	322	73,314
ChildLit	*Children Literature* (Marconi et al., 1994)	*Literature*	101	19,.370
AdLit	*Adult Literature* (Marinelli et al., 2003)	*Literature*	327	471,421
ChildEdu	*Educational Materials* for Primary School (Dell'Orletta et al., 2011a)	*Educational*	127	48,036
AdEdu	*Educational Materials* for High School (Dell'Orletta et al., 2011a)	*Educational*	70	48,103
Wiki	*Wikipedia* articles from the Italian Portal "Ecology and Environment"	*Scientific prose*	293	205,071
ScientArt	*Scientific articles* on different topics (e.g. climate changes and linguistics)	*Scientific prose*	84	471,969

Table 1: Corpora.

3 Readability Classification Across Textual Genres

In order to explore whether and to what extent readability is related to the textual genre, we carried out two sets of experiments which are aimed at discerning within each of the four genre classes easy– vs difficult–to–read documents and which differ at the level of the used models: in the first set, we used a single statistical model for all four genres, whereas in the second set the classification task was performed by using genre–specific statistical models. Achieved results have been evaluated in terms of i) overall Accuracy of the system and ii) Precision, Recall and F–measure. Accuracy is a global score referring to the percentage of correctly classified documents whereas Precision and Recall have been computed with respect to the target classes: in particular, Precision is the ratio of the number of correctly classified

Feature category	Name
Raw Text	*Average number of word for sentence* *Average number of character for word*
Lexical	*Type/Token Ratio* *Lexical density*
Morpho–syntactic	*Part-Of-Speech unigrams* *Verbal mood*
Syntactic	*Distribution of dependency types* *Depth of the whole parse tree* *Average depth of embedded complement 'chains'* *Distribution of embedded complement 'chains' by depth* *Number of verbal roots* *Arity of verbal predicates* *Distribution of verbal predicates by arity* *Distribution of subordinate vs main clauses* *Relative ordering with respect to the main clause* the *Average depth of 'chains' of embedded subordinate clauses* the *Distribution of embedded subordinate clauses 'chains' by depth* *Length of dependency links feature*

Table 2: Feature set.

documents as belonging to one target class over the total number of documents classified as belonging to the same class; Recall has been computed as the ratio of the number of correctly classified documents of a given target class over the total number of documents belonging to the same class; F–measure is the weighted harmonic mean of Precision and Recall.

In the first set of experiments, we tested three models differing at the level of the used training sets. For the first model, the training corpora for easy– and difficult–to–read documents are represented by newspaper texts, i.e. belonging to the same genre: as discussed in (Dell'Orletta et al., 2011b), this prevents interferences due to textual genre variation in the measure of text readability. For the second model, documents belonging to two different genres were selected for training: i.e. *2Par* was used as representative of the easy–to–read class, whereas for the difficult–to–read class we chose the *ScientArt* corpus. This option followed from the fact that the newspaper articles of *2Par* represent the easiest to read documents in the collection we have been dealing with, while the scientific articles included in the *ScientArt* corpus turned out to be the most difficult ones (see Section 4). For the last and third model, the training sets have been constructed by combining all the easy–to–read and difficult–to–read documents for each textual genre respectively. In Table 3, the columns headed by *2Par/Rep Model*, *2Par/ScientArt Model* and *All Easy/All Difficult Model* show the results achieved for each testual genre with the three models just described. In the last set of rows, Precision, Recall, F–measure and Accuracy scores for the whole set of documents (i.e. regardless of genre) are reported. The *2Par/Rep* model, also used in (Dell'Orletta et al., 2011b), turned out to obtain the best results. However, none of the three models achieves noteworthy results when compared with those obtained in the document readability classification task reported in (Dell'Orletta et al., 2011b) (i.e. 98.12%). This suggests that classification–based methods are able to assign a reliable readability score only when dealing with documents belonging to the same genre as the training set: see the Accuracy obtained by the *2Par/Rep* model tested on texts of the same journalistic genre (98.33%). In all other cases, the results achieved show that this method has a dramatic drop in accuracy when tested on documents belonging to different genres with respect to the training sets.

Consider now the results of the second set of experiments carried out using a specific model for each of the four genres, reported in the Column headed *Genre–specific Models* in Table 3. As expected, the overall accuracies significantly increase with respect to the results obtained by the single models. The only exception is represented by the classification of the documents in the class of *Scientific writing* characterised by a much lower Accuracy, with a Recall of

13.33% obtained in the *ScientArt* document classification and a Precision of 53.57% in the *Wiki* classification. We can hypothesize that this result follows from the internal composition of the *Wiki* training set, which does not only include easy-to-read documents with respect to the *ScientArt* class: in fact, articles concerning a specific domain in Wikipedia can also include technical (i.e. difficult–to–read) documents. With this first set of experiments, we showed that readability assessment is closely related to the textual genre of a document, suggesting that for reliably dealing with different textual genres a specific training corpus for each genre should be built. This represents a difficult objective, especially in real–world applications. In what follows, a possible alternative approach to the problem is presented, i.e. a ranking method able to reliably assign a readability score without requiring genre–specific training corpora.

	2Par/Rep Model			2Par/ScientArt Model			All Easy/All Difficult Model			Genre–specific Models		
Genre	Prec	Rec	F–measure	Prec	Rec	F–measure	Prec	Rec	F–measure	Prec	Rec	F–measure
2Par	100	96.67	98.30	50.85	100	67.41	93.55	96.67	95.08	100	96.67	98.30
Rep	96.78	100	98.36	100	3.33	6.45	96.55	93.33	94.91	96.77	100	98.36
	Accuracy: 98.33			**Accuracy: 51.67**			**Accuracy: 95**			**Accuracy: 98.33**		
ChildLit	0	0	0	46.81	73.33	57.14	100	46.67	63.63	84.61	73.33	78.57
AdLit	50	100	66.67	38.46	16.67	23.25	65.22	100	78.95	76.47	86.67	81.25
	Accuracy: 50			**Accuracy: 45**			**Accuracy:73.33**			**Accuracy: 80**		
ChildEdu	90	31.03	46.15	49.15	100	65.91	56.67	58.62	57.63	78.79	89.65	83.87
AdEdu	59.18	96.67	73.42	0	0	0	58.62	56.67	57.63	88.46	76.67	82.14
	Accuracy: 64.41			**Accuracy: 49.15**			**Accuracy: 57.63**			**Accuracy: 83.05**		
Wiki	100	20	33.33	81.25	86.67	83.87	47.17	83.33	60.24	53.57	100	69.77
ScientArt	55.55	100	71.43	85.71	80	82.76	28.57	6.67	10.81	100	13.33	23.53
	Accuracy: 60			**Accuracy: 83.33**			**Accuracy: 45**			**Accuracy: 56.67**		
TOT Easy–to–access	97.78	36.97	53.66	54.31	89.91	67.72	66.40	71.43	68.82	74.30	89.91	81.37
TOT Difficult–to–access	61.34	99.17	75.80	71.43	25	37.04	69.34	64.17	66.67	87.37	69.17	77.21
	Accuracy: 68.20			**Accuracy: 57.32**			**Accuracy: 67.78**			**Accuracy: 79.51**		

Table 3: Classification–based readability assessment results.

4 Assessing Readability Across Genres by Ranking

Our ranking–based approach to readability assessment is grounded on the notion of *cosine distance* between vectors of linguistic features (listed in Table 2). The readability score is computed as a linear combination between the distance of an analysed document (*d*) and two n–dimensional vectors representing the easy (*EV*) and the difficult–to–read poles (*DV*): $readability(d) = CosineDistance(d, EV) - CosineDistance(d, DV)$. According to the equation, the readability score ranges from -1 (easy–to–read document) to 1 (difficult–to–read document). To cope with the fact that the distance from, e.g., the easy extreme (*EV*) can express the difficulty but also the extreme readability of *d*, in the final score we combined the distance from both *EV* and *DV* poles. With respect to the ranking method proposed by (Tanaka-Ishii et al., 2010), we assign to each analyzed document a score rather than a relative ranking position, making less questionable the comprehension of the results. From the computational point of view, our method, based on the notion of *distance*, is much less complex than the (Tanaka-Ishii et al., 2010) ranking method based on a *comparison* strategy.

As stated in Section 2, we assumed the vector representing the training set of *Due Parole* as the easiest–to–read pole, while the difficult–to–read extreme was selected computing the cosine distance of the vector representing each of the eight training sets (resulting from the genre/readability combination) from the *2Par* vector. The *ScientArt* vector turned out to be the most distant one and for this reason it was chosen as the difficult extreme. We report below the ordered list of the test set vectors ranked according to their readability scores:

$$2Par < EduInf < LitInf < Rep < Wiki < LitAd < AdEdu < ScientArt$$

Note that the relative order between the easy– and difficult–to–read subclasses for each genre is preserved. It is also worth noting the ranking of *Rep* before *Wiki* which can be taken as further evidence of the difficulty of defining a readability notion valid across all genres.

Table 4 reports the ranking of all test documents based on the distance readability score. Each row represents a set of 30 documents. Interestingly, for each genre class the number of easy–to–read documents, i.e. closer to *2Par*, is higher in the top 30–document groups whereas the reverse holds in the bottom. However, the distribution of easy vs difficult to read documents is not homogeneous across genres. Consider, for instance, the easy–to–read test sets: whereas for *2Par*, *ChildLit* and *ChildEdu* the distribution across the 30–document groups follows the expectations, *Wiki* documents are homogeneously distributed in all classes. Similar observations hold in the case of the *Rep* documents for what concerns the difficult–to–read class.

	Journalism		Literature		Educational		Scientific prose	
Doc.Group	2Par	Rep	ChildLit	AdLit	ChildEdu	AdEdu	Wiki	ScientArt
0-30	15	0	4	0	8	0	3	0
31-60	6	1	11	0	9	0	3	0
61-90	4	6	7	6	3	1	1	0
91-120	1	5	1	12	2	5	4	0
121-150	2	3	2	7	5	6	4	1
151-180	1	1	2	3	2	11	4	6
181-210	1	8	2	2	1	3	5	8
211-240	0	6	1	0	0	4	4	15

Table 4: Ranking–based readability assessment results.

The results of the ranking–based readability assessment method can be used as such but can also be exploited to create genre–specific training sets which, as demonstrated in Section 3, are needed to achieve reliable results in a classification–based readability assessment task. In order to test reliability and effectiveness of our ranking method for the automatic construction of training datasets, we focused on the *Scientific writing* genre for which we obtained the most unsatisfactory results. To improve the accuracy of the classification within this class, we automatically revised the *Wiki* training set using the newly proposed distance readability score with the aim of selecting easy–to–read documents only. In particular, we ranked the documents contained in the original *Wiki* training set and picked the top list of 100 documents, which was used as the new training set. Table 5 reports the results of READ–IT with the new genre–specific model, using the automatically constructed *Wiki* training set: with respect to the previous genre–specific model, we obtained an improvement of 21.66% in Accuracy, thus demonstrating effectiveness and reliability of the proposed ranking method.

Genre	Prec	Rec	F–measure
Wiki	72.97	90	80.60
ScientArt	86.96	66.67	75.47
	Accuracy: 78.33		

Table 5: Classification results on *Scientific prose* using the automatically revised training set.

Conclusion

In this paper, we have shown that readability assessment is strongly influenced by textual genre and for this reason a genre–oriented notion of readability is needed. This represents an important requirement as far as educational applications are concerned. In particular, we demonstrated that with classification–based approaches to readability assessment reliable results can only be achieved with genre–specific models: this is far from being a workable solution, especially for less–resourced languages. We also proposed a new ranking method for readability assessment based on the notion of distance, which can be usefully exploited for automatically building genre–specific training corpora.

References

Aluisio, S., Specia, L., Gasperin, C., and Scarton, C. (2010). Readability assessment for text simplification. In *Proceedings of the 2NAACL HLT 2010 Fifth Workshop on Innovative Use of NLP for Building Educational Applications*, pages 1–9.

Attardi, G. (2006). Experiments with a multilanguage non-projective dependency parser. In *Proceedings of the Tenth Conference on Computational Natural Language Learning (CoNLL-X '06)*, pages 166–170, New York City, New York.

Dell'Orletta, F. (2009). Ensemble system for part-of-speech tagging. In *Proceedings of Evalita'09, Evaluation of NLP and Speech Tools for Italian*, Reggio Emilia, December.

Dell'Orletta, F., Montemagni, S., Vecchi, E. M., and Venturi, G. (2011a). Tecnologie linguistico–computazionali per il monitoraggio della competenza linguistica italiana degli alunni stranieri nella scuola primaria e secondaria. In Bruno, G. C., Caruso, I., Sanna, M., and Vellecco, I., editors, *Percorsi migranti: uomini, diritto, lavoro, linguaggi*, pages 319–366. McGraw–Hill.

Dell'Orletta, F., Montemagni, S., and Venturi, G. (2011b). Read-it: Assessing readability of italian texts with a view to text simplification. In *Proceedings of the the Workshop on "Speech and Language Processing for Assistive Technologies" (SLPAT 2011)*, pages 73–83, Edinburgh, July 30.

Feng, L., Jansche, M., Huenerfauth, M., and Elhadad, N. (2010). A comparison of features for automatic readability assessment. In *Proceedings of the 23rd International Conference on Computational Linguistics (COLING 2010)*, pages 276–284.

Inui, K. and Yamamoto, S. (2001). Corpus-based acquisition of sentence readability ranking models for deaf people. In *Proceedings of the Sixth Natural Language Processing Pacific Rim Symposium*, pages 159–166, Tokyo, Japan.

Kate, R. J., Luo, X., Patwardhan, S., Franz, M., Florian, R., Mooney, R. J., Roukos, S., and Welty, C. (2010). Learning to predict readability using diverse linguistic features. In *Proceedings of the 23rd International Conference on Computational Linguistics (COLING 2010)*, pages 546–554.

Ma, Y., Fosler-Lussier, E., and Lofthus, R. (2012). Ranking-based readability assessment for early primary children's literature. In *Proceedings of the 2012 Conference of the North American Chapter of the Association for Computational Linguistics: Human Language Technologies*, pages 548–552, Montréal, Canada.

Marconi, L., Ott, M., Pesenti, E., Ratti, D., and Tavella, M. (1994). *Lessico Elementare*. Zanichelli, Bologna.

Marinelli, R., Biagini, L., Bindi, R., Goggi, S., Monachini, M., Orsolini, P., Picchi, E., Rossi, S., Calzolari, N., and Zampolli, A. (2003). The italian parole corpus: an overview. In Zampolli, A. and al., editors, *Computational Linguistics in Pisa, Special Issue*, pages 401–421, XVI–XVII, Tomo I. IEPI.

Nenkova, A., Chae, J., Louis, A., , and Pitler, E. (2010). Structural features for predicting the linguistic quality of text applications to machine translation, automatic summarization and human–authored text. In E. Krahmer, M. T., editor, *Empirical Methods in NLG*, pages 222–241, Berlin Heidelberg. LNAI 5790, Springer-Verlag.

Petersen, S. E. and Ostendorf, M. (2009). A machine learning approach to reading level assessment. In *Computer Speech and Language*, pages 89–106. 23.

Piemontese, M. E. (1996). *Capire e farsi capire. Teorie e tecniche della scrittura controllata.* Tecnodid, Napoli.

Tanaka-Ishii, K., Tezuka, S., and Terada, H. (2010). Sorting texts by readability. In *Comput. Linguist.*, pages 203–227, 36, 2. MIT Press, Cambridge, MA, USA.

Štajner, S., Evans, R., Orasan, C., , and Mitkov, R. (2012). What can readability measures really tell us about text complexity? In *Proceedings of the the Workshop on Natural Language Processing for Improving Textual Accessibility (NLP4ITA)*, Istanbul, Turkey.

Author Index